# Advanced Studies in Handwriting Psychology

*COLLECTED WORKS OF ROGER RUBIN*

EDITED BY SHEILA LOWE

ISBN: 978-1-970181-55-5

Printed in the United States of America

PUBLISHING HISTORY

Write Choice Ink Ventura, California

# CONTENTS

# Foreword

Roger Rubin was in the field of advertising in the mid-1970s when he met Felix Klein and began to study graphology. Since then, he has grown into a giant in the field. He will hate reading those words because he has the humility of a Buddhist and doesn't think of himself as special, the way so many of us do.

I met Roger circa 1985 through a mutual friend. He came from New York to California to give a seminar at the San Diego chapter of the American Handwriting Analysis Foundation. I don't remember the specific topic on which he spoke, but that event was the beginning of a close and enduring friendship that has lasted for forty years. But Roger has been much more than a friend who endured many phone calls of me whining about my personal life through its major ups and downs—the kind of a friend who always answers the phone, whose shoulder is always available to cry on.

He also became the basis for the fictional character Dr. Zebediah Gold in my Forensic Handwriting suspense series. One of the memorable lines Roger supplied for Zebediah, speaking to Claudia Rose, was, "put your panties over your heart, darling."

Roger has been an important teacher and mentor, not only in my own career as a graphologist and document examiner, but for the many students who have attended his presentations at conferences around the world. He is a warm and humorous educator who teaches what handwriting and personality really means.

Those lectures were turned into monographs, which are collected in this volume. While it would be preferable to hear them live and get the fuller histories of the people behind the many handwriting samples, it is possible to learn a great deal just by reading the material. Some of these lectures were written in the distant past, and cultural views of gender roles is somewhat different than it was then. Also, more people print now than they did thirty or forty years ago, and few of these samples are printed. And yet, using the gestalt method that Roger espouses, the material can be applied to any style of writing.

I am honored that Roger has allowed me to make these lectures available to the wider audience that they deserve.

Sheila Lowe

# Character Structures and Defense Mechanisms

# Some Basic Assumptions

First there is motivation. Drives, urges, impulses such as hunger, sex, and aggression initiate patterns of action. Many sources of behavior occur outside of the individual's consciousness and are not normally acknowledged. This is the dynamic energy of unconscious mental activity. These stored mental events exert great influence on behavior both normal and abnormal. There are also principles which limit or regulate behavior. For instance, the pleasure-pain principle.: one avoids pain and pursues pleasure.

This is often contradicted in disturbed or maladaptive behaviors where the individual appears to seek out pain and reject an obvious pleasure that would benefit them. Every paranoid person has been told that his suspiciousness is unnecessary and self-defeating; compulsives have been told that their rituals are unproductive. Upon closer examination of the unconscious emotional motivations this apparent paradox confirms the pleasure principle.

The reality principle is another regulator. It is the willingness to tolerate current discomfort in order to achieve future pleasure, and it is one of the components of maturity and rational behavior. One of the fundamental assumptions of psychiatry is the model of functioning established by Sigmund Freud. This is the tripartite aspect of personality represented by the Ego, the Id, and the Superego.

The Ego includes those forces that mediate between biologically determined demands (the Id), the socially determined goals and values (the Superego) and the external demands of reality. The ego develops through the interaction of changing infantile psyche with the outer reality which really means significant other human beings..

The Ego includes both conscious and automatic unconscious processes. The conscious part is what is known as the 'self' or 'personality. The unconscious part of the ego includes the defense mechanisms and forces of repression that operate outside of an individual's awareness. We will discuss the defense mechanisms shortly.

The Id describes biologically based drives and motives such as sex, aggression, the pleasure principle, and the deep-seated need for security. Freud described the mental activity of the Id as "primary process." It is childlike, prelogical and self-centered. It is controlled by the pleasure principle and tolerates contradictions and inconsistencies. Freud also describes "secondary process" thinking which is related to the ego functions. It is rational, reality centered, and goal directed and relatively free of emotional distortions. Most thought processes combine elements of both.

The Superego deals with issues of right and wrong, good and bad. These standards develop through a child' s interaction with parental authority which create judgments, criticism, and praise for various behaviors. It also includes the "ego ideal," or the psychological representation of what a person wishes to be like, his ideal self. The Superego is also influenced by teachers, peers, and the society at large as one grows older.

### Defense Mechanisms

The Id is constantly seeking gratification of desire; the Superego is constantly censoring thoughts and behaviors. This sets up a variety of conflicts within us. How does the ego cope? How are we able to live within the bounds with all its restrictions, expectations, frustrations, and anxieties? According to Freud, the ego has a number of unconscious means of coping with frustration and warding off anxiety. These are the defense mechanisms.

### Denial of Reality

Protecting the self from the unpleasant by refusing to perceive it or face it, often by escapist activities like getting sick, fantasizing, or being preoccupied with other things.

### Displacement

Discharging pent up feelings, usually of hostility, on objects less dangerous than those which initially aroused the emotions. A child afraid of his parent's anger, shifts this fear onto being afraid of monsters at night, or zoo animals.

### Exaggeration

To make an activity, impulse, feeling, or idea extreme to defend against something unpleasant. This is closely related to denial.

### Identification

Increasing feelings of self-worth by identifying with a person, group, or institution of greater standing.

**Introjection**

Incorporating external values and standards into the ego structure so the individual is not at their mercy. If you can't beat 'em, join 'em.

**Projection**

Placing blame for difficulties on others or attributing one's own unethical desires to others.

**Reaction Formation**

Replacing a painful or unacceptable idea or feeling by its opposite. Constant cheerfulness defends against an underlying depression. Overemphasis on generosity defends against greediness. Overtly loving attitude hides underlying anger or hatred towards someone.

**Repression**

Preventing dangerous or painful thoughts from entering consciousness.

**Regression**

A return to behavior more characteristic of an earlier phase of development.

**Sublimation**

Gratification of a frustrated desire, often of a sexual nature, by a substituted activity.

**Emotional Isolation**

To operate as if emotions did not exist. To feel with the mind.

## Neurotic Character Structures

Most behaviors are the result of the tension and ensuing compromise between the demands of inner drives, feelings, attitudes, in conflict with the outer reality. Neurotic behavior is the result

of the individual' s attempt to deal with the restrictions imposed by his unconscious fears when confronted with reality situations. Neurotic symptoms, the results of this struggle, can be seen as anxiety, depression, phobias, obsessions, and somatic conversions.

The individual is often aware of these symptoms as being something outside of himself, something that feels alien to himself, very much like an infection, toothache, or a cold. This frequently leads to his seeking help to relieve the conscious distress.

Neurotic character structures are more generalized chronic behavior patterns and experience that blend rather seamlessly into the individual' s total personality so that it appears that the person and his neurotic pattern are one with each other. He seems to think in such a way and his attitudes and interests are such as to continue and sustain the neurotic process and to make the characteristic neurotic experiences inevitable.

A compulsive or obsessional type chooses not merely to be assailed by doubts and worries but goes out of his way to seek something that he can focus his worry upon.

Depressives are often not merely humiliated and victimized but seem to be on the alert for situations or persons that will continue this state of affairs.

The clusters of traits which we call character structures are extremely complex in their formation and development. They are developed during various stages of childhood and express the issues of adaptability and survival between the child's nature, or sensitivity and temperament, and the forces of reality in his environment that he had to deal with. The character structures we will address here are the Depressive, the Schizoid, the Compulsive, and the Hysteric. Other observers have used additional trait groupings and character types. They include: the Obsessive, the Phobic, the Paranoid, the Sociopathic or Impulsive types.

Each of the character structures is a grouping of traits, behaviors, responses, unconscious attitudes, and an amalgam of defense mechanisms. And each structure serves in toto to defend the person or help him survive and adjust to a given set of reality circumstances that he must deal with.

The nature of the character structure is in itself a mechanism of protection or defense. It is important to note that there is rarely an example of a 'pure' type, where an individual manifests only one character structure without some traits or behaviors from the other structures. Being able to identify the underlying character structure gives insight into the source of an individual' s basic conflicts and the developmental period in which they occurred. Since a child can be damaged or receive negative influences in any or all of the developmental periods, there is often a mixture of structures.

How these structures are formed and what purpose they serve in helping an individual adjust to his circumstances.

## Schizoid Character Structure

The Schizoid ·character structure is the earliest to develop and usually the hardest to treat therapeutically because of its remoteness and primitiveness in the developmental sequence. It is formed in the early feeding or oral period.

The child's experiences of being rejected, mishandled, loved sporadically, or being fed inconsistently or without consideration for its needs, leads to a fear of merging into a dual union or symbiotic union with the mother. But, along with the fear there is also a powerful wish for this merger.

There develops a split between good and bad objects. The experience of alternating rejection and acceptance from the mother makes her seem either all good or all bad. The feeling of comforting trust is permanently damaged. The result is rage and hostility but the child cannot express it directly so he uses the defense mechanism of projection. By creating an image of a hating other who dislikes him, the child is able to keep his own rage and anger unconscious.

By believing the other hates him, he is safe from his own wish to destroy the other. He is defended against his rage and other emotions by not feeling them directly. This protects him from the fear of isolation, abandonment, and loss of security that were established by the early mothering experiences. The schizoid's subjective emotional experience is usually diminished or flattened because of the need to fragment or deny feelings. Since he cannot clearly perceive the emotional boundaries that define him and separate out the rest of the world,, his retreat from feelings is the only safe position to take.

Submission to another is felt as a threat to his identity. The sense of being alienated protects the schizoid from feelings of vulnerability and makes withdrawal easy and comfortable as a protective device. Later in life this coping system gives the individual the ability to see things from a detached and objective point of view, because the empha-

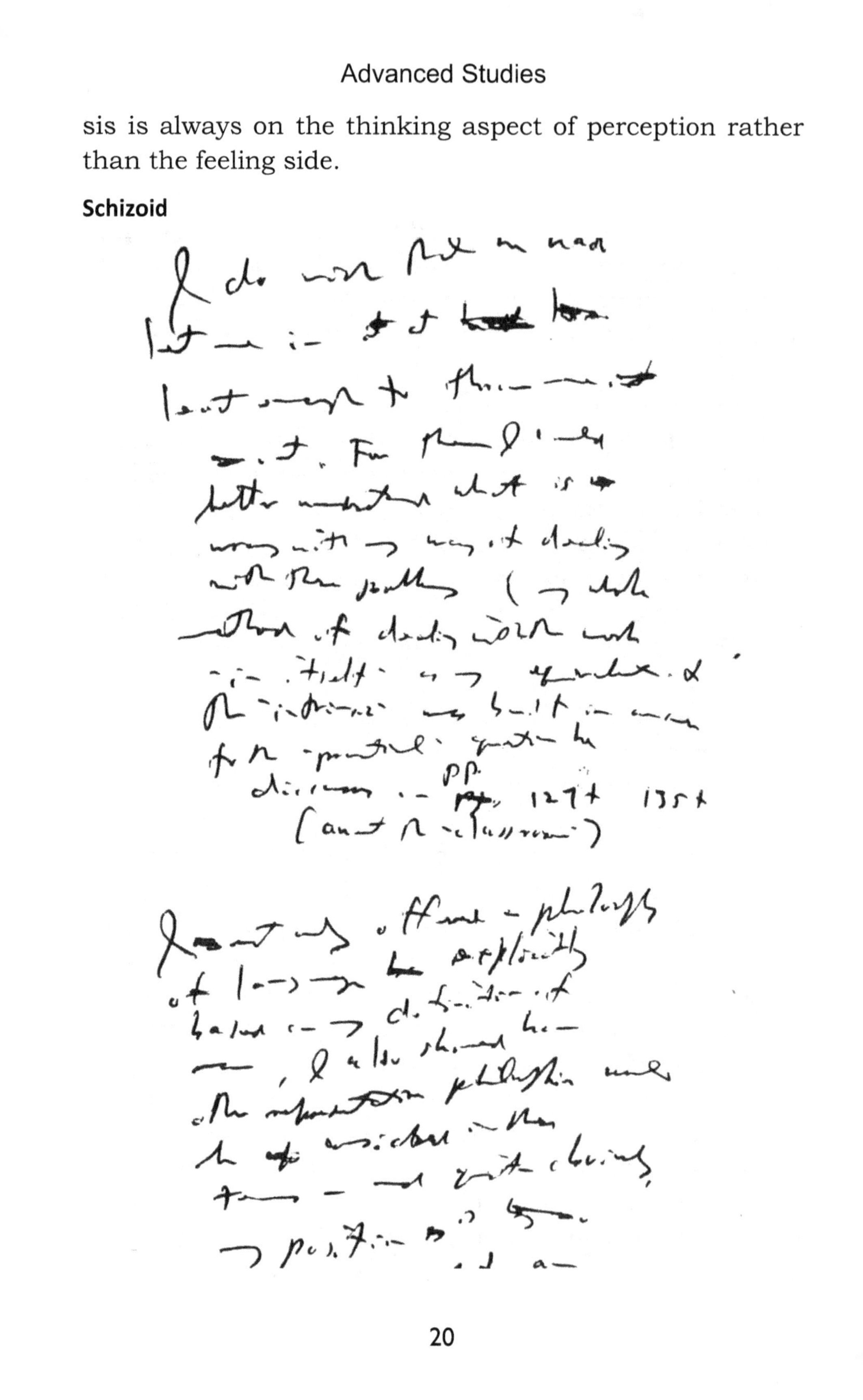

sis is always on the thinking aspect of perception rather than the feeling side.

**Schizoid**

**Schizoid**

What do you think of this as the draft
of our letter – to abt. 100 top businessmen.
Give me a call, and we'll talk it over.
Also, let this little note serve as a better
sample of my writing for analysis. I'll pay
$ I'm working on

In the past 6 months my life
has been in major upheaval on every
level. I would like to know what

Can the phoenix be found among
five and dime debris, painted ladies,
fast moving ~~fast~~ tapis.

## Depressive Character Structure

The Depressive character structure is also formed during the oral stage but it represents a higher level of emotional integration. The mother is experienced as a whole person who can be both good and bad within herself. Anxiety arises from the fear of the mother abandoning the child. This may have been brought about through difficulties in the feeding or handling process.

His narcissism and feelings of omnipotence are confronted with the reality of denial. This makes him aware of his helplessness and dependency on others. He needs his mother and she is not available.

Separation becomes the most dangerous possible threat. The child then wants to incorporate the mother into himself by "devouring" her. He then experiences the fear that his need for her will lead to her destruction.

The mother can be destroyed either through his need or his anger.Through his love the other appears, through his rage the other disappears. This creates feelings of worrying and pining away for the good object one may have destroyed which translates into guilt and self-recrimination.

When this happens, the internalized mother begins to fall apart which creates a sense of helplessness and further self-blame and guilt. But it also generates the wish to repair damage and make things good again. If only he is good enough the loved object won't leave, but if it leaves he is responsible. The underlying feeling is one of control, dependency, and anger.

When the narcissistic control pattern doesn't work there is a collapse into hopelessness and passivity. The depressive structure attempts to defend the individual against the fear of abandonment.

**Depressive**

Dear Roger —

How did I survive before you came into my life? Thank you for being you — and for always being so available and clear about life's path. I am appreciative, want to send you worlds of what You want. ---->

Dear Roger,

Enclosed is a sample of writing that I would like you to analyze - His birthdate is 12/21/28.

I have a dentist appointment at 4 o'clock on Tuesday May 31 prior to seeing you and I may

[illegible] than 5:00—

**Depressive**

17 August

Dear Roger

look forward to seeing you on Wednesday at 1 - Am full of great expectations for this year!

Best,

Paula

♀40R

Dec. 24 79

Dear Roger,

this is Xmas Eve and I hope you love as good feelings as I have. If you could have a glimpse of my day here, you would see - a house with green walls and tile floors, luscious plants, trees, flowers around, sunlight into my door; you could

♀39R

The depressive type experiences an intense desire for nearness to others. This is based on feelings of worthlessness and the need to devour the other for comfort. Passive dependencies, low self-confidence and self-esteem are characteristic of the depressive.

He feels guilty about his hostile feelings toward others but is afraid to express his anger directly. But he is also convinced that he cannot survive without the love and care of others. He turns the anger against himself because he is afraid he might destroy what he most needs. This can take the form of self-accusation, self-criticism, shame, guilt, and in extreme cases, suicide. The early attempts at repair and making good lead later to the ability to be helpful, serve, and improve the lives of others. Often there are strong empathic, and nurturing feelings which can be very useful in the more altruistic professions.

## Compulsive Character Structure

The Compulsive character structure is associated with the toilet training period, from approximately the first to the third years. This is when the child becomes, in a motoric sense, autonomous, and able to express his will. He is conscious of the difference between his will and the wishes of the adults around him. The major conflict is between obedience and defiance. Fear and rage alternate. Fear that he will be caught when naughty and punished, and rage at giving up his wishes and submitting to authority. Fear, coming from defiance leads to obedience, while rage derived from obedience leads back again to defiance.

Obedience and defiance are equated with humiliating subjugation and murderous rage. Dirt and time are the most common issues in the child's struggle with parental authority.

**Compulsive**

Myron felt inert. He stubbed his cigarette out in the ashtray and lit another one. The days prior to yesterday had been a source of inspiration to him, but since then— nothing. Sharon had called twice today and he had talked to her automatically, listening more to the traffic outside the window than to her inane monologue about Peter.

He picked up the receiver and dialed her number.

(written under duress)

Your having nice thoughts about me this morning made me feel very good. You know, when you tell me something like that, all the pressures of the moment are much easier to face. So thank you for saying it.

Much love,

## Compulsive

It has been a lovely spring day today in Islington. The birds are singing and chasing worms. The grass hasn't started to grow yet so I won't have to cut it. The daffodils and crocuses are showing off their blossoms. Time to start . . .

It's almost impossible to know what to scribble down when asked to do so randomly. Everything in England has to be done logically, and it becomes embarrassing to act in a silly way. But I like it! Is life in America more spontaneous? Let's hope so - then I'll move back. Better political system anyway, although equally conservative. More of a pioneer spirit and willingness to change, an active attitude, an adventurism - the American way. Then there's the flip side, violence, poverty, lack of concern for others, urban decay. Television is poor, culture is hard to find, etc. etc. What else to say. I should not make paragraphs, since the margins are important, no? Difficult, I'm running out of time since this must be posted off, so the writing deteriorates just as the train of thought runs out of steam! I wonder if the fact that a very dear friend has died in a rather horrible way will affect my handwriting - it has certainly affected my emotions! A dreadful disease, cancer, a modern evil. I fear it. Doesn't everybody? I wonder if it occurs more in America than in Europe. I wonder if my friend is really gone, or if she lingers near her 2-year old daughter. The grief she has felt must have been intense. She was a lovely person - truly good - rare.

I would like to stop now and go to the Post Office with this. See you on Monday - Happy New Year!

Dirt becomes associated with aggression and defiance, and defiance leads to guilty fear and the expectation of punishment.

Exposure of behaviors associated with dirt and anal functions lead to intense shame and humiliation. All behavior is viewed in terms of its competitive implications. The child's fear of authority also involves the struggle with the father or a more powerful male image and this leads to the fear of castration. The compulsive mistrusts warmth and tenderness. Emotions are connected to dependency feelings which for the compulsive suggest helplessness and that in turn stimulates fears of possible ridicule and rejection.

Pleasurable experiences are dangerous, and he cannot allow himself to enjoy himself because of unconscious guilt. He plans for future happiness but cannot enjoy it as he must always appease his conscience and control his impulses. The compulsive position is one of defense against impulses that are too powerful and are forbidden and therefore dangerous. He demonstrates a powerfully primitive and punitive superego to keep himself controlled and in line, The price paid for avoiding fear and rage is loneliness, social isolation, and a lowered capacity for pleasure. He tends to reason out his feelings and engage people on level of theories, concepts, situations, and details. All this to avoid connecting on the level of feeling and emotion.

Rigidity of thinking and emotional isolation protect him against his primitive forbidden impulses. In seeking to recreate the original omnipotent relationship with his mother the compulsive type can establish a similar alliance with a system of thought, a religion, or a scientific doctrine. The compulsive's concentration, willpower, determination, and single mindedness can lead to significant achievements, especially in areas that are intensively routine or technical.

## Histrionic Character Structure

The histrionic character structure occurs latest in the developmental sequence, during the fourth and fifth years, and it is much more common in girls than boys. In the early infantile struggles over sleeping and feeding and being held, the child discovers that dramatic scenes lead to getting her way.

As she grows older, she learns to get her way by playing the parents off against each other. She also learns to escape punishment by being sick, upset, saying she is sorry or "feels bad." The child does not experience the consequences of misbehavior, and is left with unresolved feelings of guilt as a result of escaping punishment thereby interfering with the normal development of conscience.

The typical mother of the histrionic is competitive and unresponsive on deeper emotional levels. The mother will overindulge or overprotect to compensate for her inability to give real love. She will show warmth most often when the child is ill, depressed, or emotionally upset. Later in life, this establishes depression, physical illness, and tantrums as the means of getting dependent care from others.

The child's need to maintain a dependent relationship with her mother makes it difficult for her to mature. An internalized ego ideal is never established. Instead, she comes to rely on approval from others to maintain her self-esteem. She will see the father as a maternal substitute.

**Histrionic**

[...]rote sometimes because I am unable to play an [...]strument or write music.

I am capable of creating with my [...]ad guitarist—Jimmy Crespo—we [...] capable of spontaneity (I didn't spell the [...]

think that I'm open and giving, I'm shown how much more so I can be. The most frightening aspect of cutting through the layers of shit is seeing how many and how thick they are. And with Lynnie the layers are forever being exposed. [Three days later]: I'm enclosing Patti Smith's

**Histrionic**

I have been very damp + chilly today + my chest is beginning to hurt — I hope it stops raining!

OK I forgot to mail it while I was there — But I still wanted you to know this magical place reminded me of you — love [illegible]

Typically, the father is emotionally ambivalent toward the child. He is there occasionally to save her from punishment and console her, but he is frequently absent and unavailable. The rejections from the father leave the child feeling that she has no one.

Her rage may take the form of emotional outbursts and demanding behavior or increased seductiveness and manipulativeness. Self-dramatization, simulated compliance, seductiveness, and physical illness are used to establish control with her father. She can't give up her attachment to him, and yet her sexual attachment to him. is too threatening due to the Oedipal fears. So, her response is to repress her sexuality and true intensity of feeling because it is too overwhelming for her to bear.

The histrionic position with its diffusion, distractibility, excess of affect, unfocused impressionability, fantasy, and pseudo emotions defends the individual against the reawakening of repressed sexual impulses and the consequent intensity of feelings.

Repression is the basic defense mechanism. It can lead to the classical conversion symptoms such as blindness, paralysis, or amnesia. Intense emotionality defends against deeper feelings. Superficial warmth and seductiveness, especially with the opposite sex, prevent real feelings of closeness and the vulnerability to rejection. The hysteric type will not be interested in details, organization, and f actual data. Instead, they are attracted to the vivid, the colorful, the emotionally charged and the emotionally provocative.

They are theatrical and dramatic and are interested in the impression they make while remaining innocently unaware of the consequences of their behavior.

## Depressive Character Structure

—*Desire for nearness*

—*Desire for submission*

—*Incapable of genuine partnership*

—*Lack of ego power*

—*Feeling at the mercy of others*

—*Feeling of being asked to do too much (resignation)*

—*No desire for planning*

—*No courage*

—*Guilt Feelings*

—*Seemingly unassuming*

—*Fear of self-development*

—*Fear of isolation*

—*Fear of losses*

But also:

—*Empathy*

—*Helpfulness*

—*Devoted*

—*Grateful*

—*Subordination*

## Compulsive Character Structure

—*Cannot tolerate changes*

—*Safeguarding*

—*Obstinacy*

—*Intolerance*

—*Dogmatism*

—*Tendency toward principles*

—*Pondering*

—*Caution*

—*Retain prejudice*

—*Attachment to traditions*

—*Fear of change of conduct*

—*Fear of the transitory*

**But also:**

—*Ambitions*

—*Diligent*

—*Sense for duty*

—*Perseverance*

—*Firmness*

—*Seriousness*

## Histrionic Character Structure

—*No acknowledgment of order and rules*

—*No relationship to outside world*

—*Rejection of responsibility*

—*Infantile*

—*No self-criticism*

—*No endurance*

—*No concentration*

—*Lack of patience*

—*Looking for admiration*

—*Curious*

—*Spontaneity*

—*Lives in a pseudo-world*

—*Short attention span*

—*Refuses to recognize obligation*

—*More initiative than persistence*

—*Enemy of traditions*

—*Fear of reality and necessity*

—*Seeks artificial nearness*

But also:

—*Ready to take chances*

—*Flexible*

—*Impulsive*

—*Optimistic*

## Schizoid Character Structure

—*Strives toward self-development*

—*Egocentric attitude*

—*Autism*

—*Rationalism*

—*Emphasis on intellect rather than emotion*

—*Fear of obligations*

—*Few social contacts*

—*Rejecting*

—*Distrustful, skeptical, cynical*

—*Abrupt change of affect (reactions)*

—*Change between over and underestimating self*

—*Fear of nearness*

—*Fear of submission and adaptation (regarded as loss of identity)*

—*Fear of each new start*

But also:

—*Independence, objectivity, sense of criticism*

—*No traditions*

—*No sentimentality*

—*Uncompromising*

The above lists are reprinted with the kind permission of Felix Klein

## BIBLIOGRAPHY

Freud, Anna - *Ego and Mechanisms of Defense.* Int'l University Press, 1946

Klein, Felix - *Character Structure of Neuroses.* Monograph, 1974

MacKinnon, - R.A. and Michaels, R. *The Psychiatric Interview in Clinical Practice.* Phil., PA.: W .B. Saunders Co., 1971

Matheson, D.W . - *Introductory Psychology.* Dryden Press, 1975

Segal, Hannah - *Introduction to Melanie Klein.* Basic Books, 1964.

Shapiro, David - *Neurotic Styles.* Basic Books, 1965.

# Attachments: the Effect of the Infant-Mother Bond

# Attachments

# The effect of the infant-mother bond

Understanding the infant-mother bond ranks as one of the most important areas of exploration in modem psychology. It is one that has a widespread and deep importance because it holds so many clues to how we become who we are. Until the last two decades nothing could be said with scientific authority about almost any dimension of the infant-mother bond. No one had studied how aspects of relatedness, good and bad, are transmitted. What does a child need, at minimum, in order to feel that the world of people is a positive place and that he has value.

What experiences in infancy will enable him to feel confident enough to explore and develop healthy relationships and to be capable of rebounding from adversity. Today, mothers are spending less and less time in the home. Families are falling apart and are being regrouped in new combinations. Debates are raging about the emotional needs of school children and the value of day care.

Understanding the basic structures of the infant-mother connection and their effect in later life periods has a social as well as a psychological urgency.

As recently as fifty years ago, Arnold Gesell, an American pediatrician and developmental psychologist, first brought attention to the child's inborn maturational timetable. He also reflected the ideas of the eugenics movement. They believed that the infant is, in essence, a genetic construct. The way children turn out is essentially predetermined by heredity and not by the way they are raised. On the opposite side of the spectrum were the behaviorists who thought that children were entirely products of their environment. John Watson, a psychologist, believed, as stated in his widely read book on child rearing, that the mother's affection was potentially dangerous to the child's character. Picking up a child when it cried or feeding it on demand were pernicious forms of coddling.

An alternate position was taken by psychoanalysts. They accepted certain aspects of the hereditary makeup, especially the strength of the sexual and aggressive drives. But most analysts saw the infant-mother relationship as being important to healthy emotional development. Among them was John Bowlby, a British psychoanalyst, born in 1907.

Bowlby was part of a mid-century trend that was moving away from seeing people as isolated energy systems and seeing them as embedded in relationships. His important thinking and work began evolving in the late thirties when he was influenced by the work of ethologists, such as Konrad Lorenz, who did experiments with animal infant-mother bonding. Bowlby concluded that humans also possess bonding behaviors and inter-generational cues.

That we are in some way prewired for some kind of relational experience. He later worked with children and adolescents and his observations at that time were powerful determinants in his theory of the effect of early infant and childhood separations on the developing personality. His paper, "Forty Four Juvenile Thieves: Their Characters and Home Life", published in 1944 noted that all the juveniles had severely depriving separations from their mothers at a very early age. As a result, none of the children had a chance to develop true attachments, and none were able to make any later attachment. He believed that this was the basis for their severely sociopathic behaviors.

Bowlby's ideas were derived from observation and brilliant theorizing about the nature of relationships that originate and derive from early infant-mother attachment experiences. The psychoanalytic thinking of his time cared little for the reality of the child's or patients experience. It was more absorbed in the theories of the intrapsychic and fantasy life. This brings to mind Freud's rejection of his patient's claims of having been sexually abused or victims of incest as children.

He originally believed them but later revised his theory to suggest that these experiences were fantasy projections or wishful thinking, and was an aspect of the Oedipal conflict rather than a difficult, and painful real life experience. Bowlby's most notable achievement was the exploration of infant mother attachments, developed over the course of three decades and culminating in the publishing of his now famous three volume series, "Attachment'," "Separation," "'Loss, Sadness and Depression."

## Core themes

One of Bowlby's core themes was that the baby is wired to create attachments from the mother to itself and then is also pre-programmed to respond to the attachment signals and behaviors of the mother. The primary purpose of many of the infants and young child's instinctual responses, in man as in other animals, is to insure proximity to the adult, a necessity for survival. Sucking, clinging, following, crying, and smiling are instinctual responses which form a mosaic of attachment behavior. Crying and smiling do not actively attach the child to the parent, rather they attach the parent to the child. A short time after, the child develops clinging and following behaviors to assure proximity. These reach a peak during the second year. Anxiety, illness, fear, and fatigue will cause a child to increase these attachment behaviors. Bowlby believed that neurotic disturbances arise out of distortions of the attachment system.

Maternal behaviors that cause a child to feel hostile toward it's mother, such as minor rejections or short separations, may also intensify the child's following and clinging. This can later lead to neurotically dependent behavior patterns. When the mother figure is massively rejecting or totally absent, attachment behaviors may fail to mature or become totally repressed. This deadening of affect and expectation of warmth and care created detachment, and therefore, was the most important underlying issue in sociopathy.

Bowlby believed that in childhood the primary caretaker is crucial to healthy development. Maternal deprivation and separation in the early years cause the attachment response and its emotional and developmental potentials to become disrupted. Given this natural predisposition, even a threat to abandon a child who misbehaves, or a threat to send him away, or threats by a mother to kill herself are terrifying to a child.

They can generate unbearable levels of anxiety and lead to later dysfunctions. Bowlby felt that separation from the mother or mothering figure brought about three primary responses that are key to understanding human psychology. First comes protest and anger, which is the embodiment of the separation anxiety. Next is despair, an Indication of mourning. Last is detachment, which is a form of defense.

Separations, in extreme cases, such as in children who suffered long hospitalizations, lead to a detached, affectionless psychopathy, which is a type of pathological mourning. It is dangerous because it seals the personality not only from despair but from love and anything that could counter feelings of worthlessness, guilt, and bitter mistrust. Less severe depriving separations in infancy show up when the child faces losses later in life. He will be prone to separation anxiety and depressive episodes as well.

Bowlby's theory claimed that the responsiveness of parents to their infants' attachment signals and their availability in stressful situations provide infants with a secure base on which to organize expectations about the world and to handle distress. Infants of responsive parents react to separation with less fear, hostility, and avoidance than those of non-responsive parents.

They also show more exploratory behavior, better problem solving as toddlers and more ego resiliency in preschool age. He wrote and encouraged parents to stay closely connected with their babies at least until the age of three in order to form the best possible attachment base. Theorists in the field of child development, as well as feminists, often attacked his ideas. They are still being debated today but with a good deal less rancor, as much of his thinking is now widely accepted.

**Mary Ainsworth**

His theories lacked validating studies to support them until the ground breaking work of Mary Ainsworth in the late 60s and 70s. Her major contribution flowed from an ingenious experimental design called the "Strange Situation." It was the only psychological test up until that time that measured relatedness interactions rather than individual behaviors. No one before had found a way to assess how a style of parenting affected individual differences. The original research used twelve month old babies and was designed to measure the child's reaction to an inherently stressful strange situation. It consisted of a series of episodes covering a period of twenty minutes and taking place in room with three chairs, a bunch of toys on the floor, and a one way mirror for observation.

Episode one was a very brief introduction. Episode two-the baby alone in the playroom with its mother. Episode three-a stranger enters the room Episode four-mother leaves the room but the stranger remains. Episode five-the mother returns and the stranger slips out. Episode six—the mother leaves and the baby is entirely alone. Episode seven—stranger returns and attempts to comfort the baby. Episode eight-the mother returns.

Ainsworth's expectations based on prior research and observation in Uganda and Baltimore was largely fulfilled and went as follows: Although it was a strange environment almost all the babies began to explore but keeping visual tabs on mother as well. Exploration diminished when the stranger arrived, with the babies spending more time looking at the stranger than at the toys. They were wary, but the pleasant stranger managed to get at least one smile from half the babies.

When the mother walked out of the room for the first time, half the babies cried at some point. A large minority of the babies were lured back into play by the stranger, but a few who were truly distressed could be fully comforted by her. When mother returned, a vast majority of babies greeted her by smiling, vocalizing, or crying, or more often, with some combination of reactions.

About half wanted physical contact, the majority achieving it within 15 seconds. When the mother slipped out a second time, leaving the baby completely alone in the room, the distress was usually very intense, with most of the babies crying, many of them so pitifully that the episode had to be curtailed. When the stranger returned, she did not have much success in comforting the babies who were distressed. Many of them did accept her soothing, and, although still upset seemed to derive some comfort from contact with her.

The babies' responses to her efforts to get them to play were mixed. When the mother returned the second time, the great majority of babies greeted her in some way, often with intensified crying. More than twice as many achieved contact with her within fifteen seconds of her return than in the previous reunion, and almost all of them were picked up, as had been recommended. Almost half the babies avoided the mother in some way in the last episode, most prominently by turning away from her.

The results from the Strange Situation assessments and other studies based on extensive in home interviews and observations led Ainsworth to formulate three different kinds of attachments between infants and mothers—the securely attached, the ambivalently / anxiously attached, and the avoidantly attached.

Ainsworth also developed four scales to rate a mother's way of being with their baby. How often was the mother sensitive to her infant's signals? How much acceptance of the baby did she demonstrate as opposed to rejection? Did she cooperate with the baby's desires and rhythms, or did she tend to interfere, imposing her own schedule and pace in feeding, handling, and playing? How available was she and how often did she ignore her baby?

Mothers of the securely attached children were responsive to their infant 's signals, quick to pick them up when they cried, inclined to hold them longer and with more apparent pleasure. They were rated high in sensitivity, acceptance, and emotional accessibility. A high score in the maternal rating seemed to be the key to a secure attachment. The mother of the two insecure groups rated equally low on all four scales with the main difference being that, while the mothers of ambivalent children were often maddeningly unpredictable, mothers of avoidant children were substantially more rejecting and were more averse to physical contact.

Securely attached, are the children who sought their mother when distressed, who seemed confident of her availability, who were upset when she left them, who eagerly greeted her upon her return, and who warmly accepted and were readily comforted by her soothing embrace.

Ambivalently attached, are the children who tended to be the most overtly anxious, who, as with the avoidant babies, were also clingy and demanding at home, who were also upset when abandoned by the mother in the Strange Situation, but who, despite wanting her desperately when she returned, arched away, or went limp in her embrace, so that they could not be soothed.

Avoidantly attached, are the children who seemed to depend less on their mother as a secure base, who sometimes attacked her with a random act of aggression, who were far more clingy and demanding than the secure children in the home environment, and who, despite in some cases being just as openly upset by the mother's departure in the Strange Situation, showed no interest in her when she returned.

Ainsworth's work set off a flood of research using the Strange Situation to correlate the attachment and parenting styles with the child's character development, schoolwork, problem solving ability, self-reliance, self-esteem, peer relations, and general sociability.

### Alan Sroufe

Alan Sroufe, at the University of Minnesota, worked with toddlers and preschool children in the Strange Situation test and found that the securely attached children did better in almost every respect compared to the anxious or avoidant children. They were able to manage their impulses and desires more flexibly as well as handle stress without falling apart, as did the ambivalent ones. The secure group showed more enthusiasm, more cooperation, more persistence, more responsiveness to instruction, and less frustration. They were rated higher in display of positive feelings.

None of the ambivalent children smiled, laughed, or expressed delight at the same level, and almost half of the avoidant children engaged in prominent displays of pouting, whining, and hitting. Sroufe identified three types of avoidant children at this age–the lying bully who blames others; the shy, spacey loner who seems emotionally flat; and the obviously disturbed child who daydreams and shows little interest in his environment. He also named two ambivalent patterns–the fidgety, impulsive child with poor concentration who is tense and easily upset by failures; and the fearful, hypersensitive, clingy child who lacks initiative and gives up easily.

The teachers of these children tend to treat the securely attached in warm, matter-of-fact, age appropriate ways; to indulge, excuse and infantilize the clingier, more scattered ambivalent children; and to be controlling and angry with the avoidant children, despite their being equally needy.

The insecurely attached child whether aggressive or cloying, puffed up or easily deflated tries the patience of peers and adults, alike. They elicit reactions that repeatedly reconfirm the child's, and later, the adult's distorted view of the world. These patterns are an underlay that tend to persist into and through adulthood and can be seen as profoundly influencing the course and quality of a lifetime. They become solidified with age.

During their early years insecurely attached children are believed to be somewhat amenable to change. Research has shown that if they are securely attached to their father or another secondary care giver, it is the best insurance in helping to overcome the insecure attachment to the mother. Even if it's only someone they see occasionally, the knowledge that he is cared about keeps a different model of relatedness alive in him and can form the basis of overcoming adversity.

Research done by Jeffery Simpson of Texas A & M, has dealt with attachment styles and romantic relationships. He has found that people who possess a secure attachment style develop mental models of themselves as being friendly, good-natured, and likable, and of significant others as generally being well-intentioned, reliable, and trustworthy. They are able to get close to others, and are comfortable depending on others and having others depend on them.

They don't worry about being abandoned or someone being too emotionally close to them. They experience relatively high levels of trust, commitment, and interdependence in relationships. Those who display an anxious style develop models of themselves as being misunderstood, lacking in confidence, and underappreciated, and of significant others as being unreliable and unwilling to commit to permanent relationships. They exhibit considerable ambivalence toward romantic partners.

Even though they may yearn to develop stable, supportive relationships, their insecurity about the stability of relationships in general precludes them from experiencing high levels of trust, commitment. interdependence and satisfaction. They are very concerned about issues concerning their partner's predictability and dependability.

Those who have an avoidant style develop models of themselves as being suspicious, aloof, and skeptical of significant others as being basically unreliable or overly eager to commit themselves to relationships. They develop emotionally distant relationships defined by lower levels of trust, interdependence, commitment, and satisfaction. Avoiding excessive intimacy is one of their main concerns.

Studies by C. Hazan and P. Shaver in 1987 through a self-disclosure method evaluated the different attachment styles and success in the workplace. As expected the securely attached were doing quite well in terms of achievement and satisfaction. The ambivalents had the lowest average income and the most problems in performance. They tended to procrastinate, had difficulty concentrating, and were most distracted by interpersonal concerns. The avoidants were most likely to be workaholics and were most inclined to let work interfere with their social life. Their incomes were on a par with the securely attached.

Severe disruptions of early attachments such as prolonged maternal deprivation, harsh separations, and/or the death of a primary attachment figure can lead to the development of serious disorders, including agoraphobia, depression, psychopathic personality type. Bowlby believed that avoidant attachment lay at the core of the narcissistic personality disorder.

The young child whose mother has not attuned to him feels unknown and unappreciated. He shrinks back into a feeling of helplessness, smallness, defectiveness, and shame which he may defend by clinging to his infantile grandiosity. He can grow into an adult who seeks the adulation and perfect union he never knew as an infant. Outwardly self-important, self-adoring, and acting as if entitled, inside he is haunted by a fragile self-esteem.

Avoidant attachment is a likely component of the compulsive personality type. It would be seen in the avoidant child's narrowing of his focus to a toy or some other object to escape his painful conflicts and deprivations.

Ambivalent attachment may underlie the histrionic (hysterical) character structure. Histrionics tend to be scattered, charmingly incompetent, and easily thrown by schedules, details, and responsibilities. Although socially popular, they flee from intimacy and tend to be demanding, clingy, immature and easily overwhelmed by their own emotions.

Early ambivalence may also be connected to the borderline personality type. They are impulsive, needy, rageful and self-destructive. They are preoccupied with attachment signals as they seem to say "do you really care for me," "I'm going to make you prove it," ""you've turned against me," "I'm utterly alone and unwanted."

These brief comments barely touch the surface of what is going on in developmental psychology as a result of Bowlby's and Ainsworth's pioneering work. Attachment theory labeling, exploring the blurry areas where attachment theory doesn't quite fit, explaining how individuals are able to find positive attachment figures and deal with and often surmount their infant bonding problems are a few of the areas of research.

Robert Karen has written: "We cannot change our childhood. But we can let go of the defensive and obsessive postures formed at that time. We can make sense of what has been repressed and forgotten.

We can re-experience dissociated feelings with a new appreciation for ourselves as we were as children, for the situation that existed at that time, for the parents who may have caused us to suffer. And we can successfully mourn our losses. If we've managed to hold on to an alternative model, and if we are wise or lucky in love, we may be able to work through our childhood experience in the context of a marriage or something like it.

In either case, if we remain conscious of ourselves and of the pull of early models, even if hang ups of various kinds remain, as inevitably they must, we have a better chance of creating satisfying relationships with our mates and secure relationships with our children. To that extent it seems that in emotional life, much as in history, we are only doomed to repeat what has not been remembered, reflected upon, and worked through."

| **Securely Attached** | **Avoidantly Attached.** | **Ambivalently Attached.** |
|---|---|---|
| Mother (or primary caregiver) is warm, sensitively attuned, consistent. Quickly responds to baby's cries. | Mother is often emotionally unavailable or rejecting. Dislikes neediness, may applaud independence. | Mother is unpredictable or chaotic. Often attentive but out of sync with baby. Most tuned in to baby's fear. |
| Baby readily explores, using mother as secure base. Cries least of three groups, most compliant with mother, and most easily put down after being held. | By end of first year, baby seeks little physical contact with mother, randomly angry with her, unresponsive to being held, but often upset when put down | Baby cries a lot, is clingy and demanding, often angry, upset by small separations, chronically anxious in relation to mother, limited in exploration. |
| *Strange Situation*: Actively seeks mother when distressed, maintains contact on reunion, readily comforted. | *Strange Situation*: Avoids mother when distressed, seems blasé. | *Strange Situation:* Difficult to soothe after separation; angry and seeking comfort simultaneously. |
| *Preschool:* Easily makes friends. Popular. Flexible and resilient under stress. Spends more time with peers. Good self esteem. | *Preschool*: Often angry, aggressive, defiant. May be isolated, disliked. Hangs around teachers. Withdraws when in pain. | *Preschool:* fretful and easily overwhelmed by anxiety. Immature, overly dependent on teacher. May be victimized by bullies. |

| **Securely Attached** | **Avoidantly Attached** | **Ambivalently Attached.** |
|---|---|---|
| Teachers in warm, matter-of-fact, age-appropriate ways. | Teachers become controlling and angry. | Teachers indulge, excuse, and infantilize. |
| *Age 6 with parents:* Warm and enthusiastic. Able to be open and to engage in meaningful exchanges. Comfortable with physical contact. | *Age 6 with parents:* Abrupt, neutral, unenthusiastic exchanges. Absence of warm physical contact. | *Age 6 with parents*: Mixes intimacy seeking with hostility. Affectedly cute or ingratiating. May be worried about mother when apart. |
| *Middle childhood.* Forms close friendships, and is able to sustain them in larger peer groups. | *Middle childhood:* No close friends or friendships marked by exclusivity, jealousy. Often isolated from the group. | *Middle childhood:* Trouble functioning in peer groups. Difficulty sustaining friendships when in larger group. |
| **Secure Adult** | **Dismissive Adult** | **Preoccupied Adult** |
| Easy access to wide range of feelings and memories, positive and negative. Balanced view of parents. If secure in childhood, has worked through hurt and anger. | Dismissing of importance of love and connection. Often idealizes parents, but actual memories don't corroborate. Shallow, if any, self-reflection. | Still embroiled with anger and hurt at parents. Unable to see own responsibility in relationships. Dreads abandonment. |
| Usually has securely attached child | Usually has avoidantly attached child. | Usually has ambivalently attached child. |

# Advanced Studies

# Getting Under the Mask: Persona Handwriting

# GETTING UNDER MASK
# PERSONA HANDWRITING

The Persona as a psychological concept was first formulated by Carl Jung and refers to the mask that the individual must wear in his or her daily intercourse in society. The word itself was derived ran the ancient Greeks in their theatrical productions indicating the mask the actor wore over his face which would give the audience the immediate recognition of his character and the person or stylized role he was enacting.

Jung's idea is that the individual is never able to meet his fellow human beings with the totality of his personality, that is, his combined consciousness and unconscious.

He cannot present these all at once because he does not have them all in control at a given time. So, in particular social relationships the individual develops specific parts of his personality according to the situation and according to the other individuals with whom he is in contact.

It turns out that one can have many personalities, many sides to his life, in proportion to the number of different life situations one confronts. One is a child to his mother, a lover to his sweetheart, a boss to his employee, a teacher to his student, etc., etc. In some situations, one's persona will show affection, in others meekness, in others forgetfulness depending on his social relationships and the need for appropriate response. The Persona involves our habits of personal appearance, posture, gait, dress, facial expression, the quality of our smile and our frown, even our way of wearing our hair.

Society requires easy classifications, and the individual in turn seeks to create a mask to make these classifications possible. The Persona, in Jung's view, becomes identified with the Ego rather than the Self.

The Self is the personality as a whole, whereas the Ego or Ego-complex is that part of the Self that contains the field of consciousness or the condition of consciousness. So, the Persona representing conscious attitudes is placed in the psyche, in Jung's view, as the opposite to the unconscious. We tend to develop our stronger sides and make them more conscious and turn them into a persona-mask.

But the weaker, unadapted side falls back into the unconscious, to the less visible side of the personality, its darker side. Jung called it the "shadow" because it is hidden and has a sinister uncontrolled role in our lives. The Persona and the Shadow are polar opposites. An individual using the Persona in a healthy way is using it flexibly, appropriately, and as a variable cover in various life situations.

There are those for whom the inner or personal reality of creative and dream expression is so threatening or so forbidden that they must hide this side away from view so that neither they nor others can see within.

For these individuals the Persona is a false self-defense, a suit of armor, like a mask that is wearing a person. It protects the true self, which has been traumatized and deeply injured, from further injury. The Persona defense is a coping system that staves off and denies depression or the possibility of a psychic breakdown.

D.W. Winnicott, a psychoanalyst has written about depression as evidence of personal integration because it shows the willingness to experience guilt, pain, and sadness more directly and it suggests a potential for resolving the psychological distress because of that greater willingness to confront the realities of the true self.

See illustrations #1, #2 and #3 on the following pages for examples of this.

**Illustration #1**. Female. Age 52. RH.Narrow letters, tight space between letters, wide space between words, restricted rightward movement reveal emotional inhibition, no contact with feelings, denial of inner reality. Strokes moving upward and to the right are a contrived show of cheerfulness and a superficial upbeat manner.

I like this card?
thought you would!

Have a happy day Michael
and enjoy yourself
Love from your
Mum and Dad.

**Illustration #2.** Male. Age 30. RH. Japanese background. Works with crafts. Emphasis on form but contrived rather than developed. Narrowness and rigidity mean excessive control and formality. Right slant shows need for contact, while the constricted forms deny it. The bottom sample is an enlargement of part of the top.

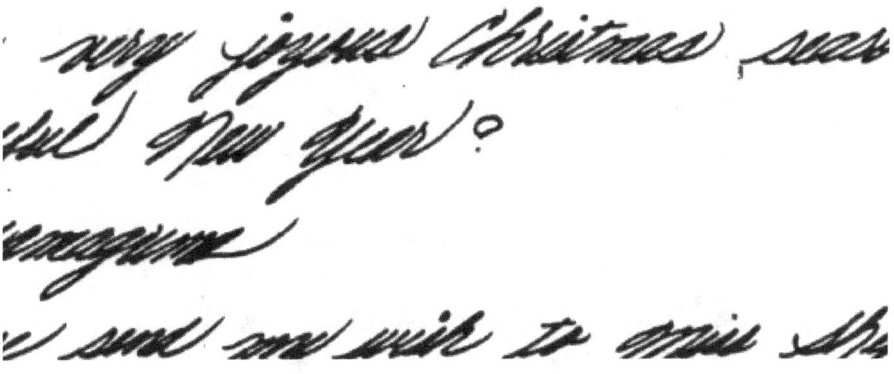

**Illustration #3.** Female. Age 55. Concert pianist. Mechanical perfectionist. Emotional isolation is seen in huge space between words. Her strict rules don't allow for growth and development. A frozen writing.

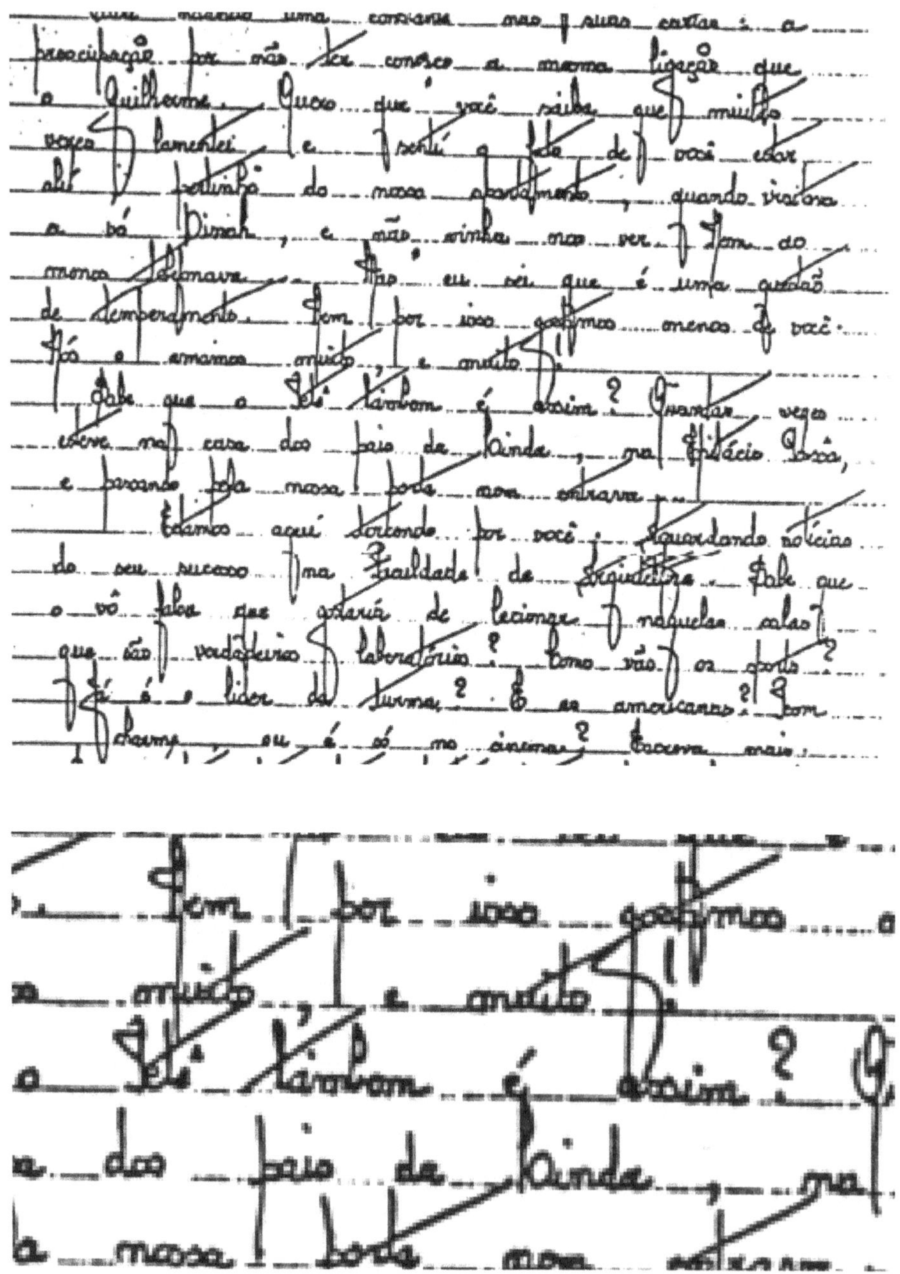

One of the most common of the Persona defenses is what might be called the "Good Girl Syndrome." This syndrome occurs. When the nurturant parent lacks attunement to the child's needs, and demands that the child live up to the expectations of the parent. The child feels deep fear that it will not be fed or loved or be attended to unless it conforms to the wishes of the parent at the expense of its own desires. An existential anxiety develops based on fear of deprivation and denial of care. "If I don't conform, I will be pushed out into the cold and die." The child decides to be "good" by living up to the expectations of the parents, by behaving as if she were happy.

Learned emotional control, holding back present gratification for future rewards, suppression of anger, compliance, achieving goals to prove her value to the parents and pleasing them, doing things well to the point of being a perfectionist, fear of criticism, guilt at errant behavior, all these are the hallmarks of the "Good Girl." Of course, she is never good enough. There is always something not quite right with her performance. She is not good or perfect enough to win the love she seeks. That is the old "carrot and the stick" routine that keeps motivating her to do even more and to continue to be good.

Her parents emphasize the outside at the expense of the inside, i.e. aggression and sexuality. Genuine expression of aggression and sexuality is dangerous and is penalized, even killed. The fundamental error the "Good Girl" makes is to equate the world to the parents. The persona of the Good Girl allows the true self to survive but it goes into exile. She is defended against feelings of depression and rage. In some cases, it is so effective and rigidly constructed that it remains immovable for an entire lifetime. Solid armor plating. The anger out in the form of the projection defense. She will be critical of others in the very same terms that she was criticized. She incorporates the conventional attitudes of her parents. Since nothing new can get through there is very low potential for growth. She can't face the vulnerability or letting go. See illustrations #4 and #5.

**Illustration #4**. Female. Age 26. RH. Extremely rigid school type writing. Roundedness suggests a feeling nature which is held in check by the rigidity of form. Conventional, conservative, and tearful. The oral hooks reflect attachment to the past and to the unfulfilled needs in early childhood.

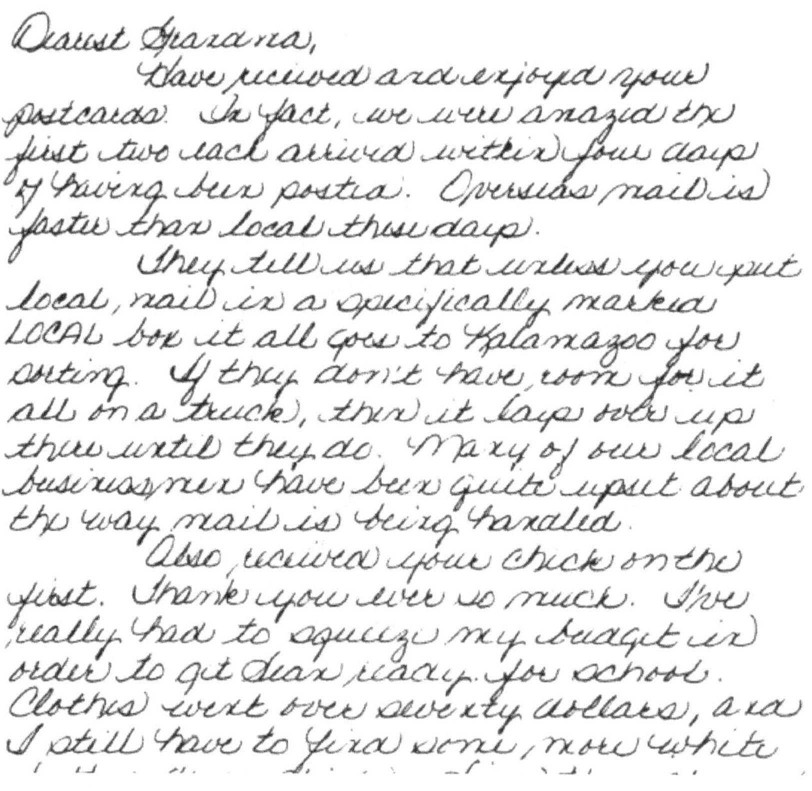

Dearest Grandma,

Have received and enjoyed your postcards. In fact, we were amazed the first two each arrived within four days of having been posted. Overseas mail is faster than local these days.

They tell us that unless you put local mail in a specifically marked LOCAL box it all goes to Kalamazoo for sorting. If they don't have room for it all on a truck, then it lays over up there until they do. Many of our local businessmen have been quite upset about the way mail is being handled.

Also received your check on the first. Thank you ever so much. I've really had to squeeze my budget in order to get Dean ready for school. Clothes went over seventy dollars, and I still have to find some more white

**Illustration #5**. Female. Age 36. RH. Always serving needs of others, proving she is "good" and worthy of love. Rounded forms, uneven base line, and garland connection show warmth, feeling, and strong mood swings. Space picture and overlapping lines (zonal interference) show inner confusion and dependencies.

I have enclosed handwriting of
three people – my father, his wife
(Kathy) & my good friend Lois.
I will be leaving for Europe
on the 30th and I'm feeling
pressured by my clients &, I guess,
life in general. I want to use
the 2 1/2 weeks I'll be gone to clear
my head & consider what my
next career move should be. hence
my desire to see you before I go.
Looking forward to seeing you
on the 30th.

Then there is the Good Girl who is a flip-flop type. Every Good Girl is holding in a large reservoir of anger and potential rebellion. She will find a way to act out what has been forbidden by doing it behind the backs of her parents or husband or boss or any authority figure. She will go out with a man of a different race or social level, take drugs, wear extreme clothes, be sexually promiscuous or adventurous, and act out anti-social impulses. Yet, all the while, acting conventionally and seeming to conform to the expectation of her parents or social group. Some may go along or many years in a conforming pattern, then unexpectedly act out their anger. Nuns who leave their order after many years of obedience in a sudden expression of dissatisfaction with the system would be a good example. Often it is only this rage and rebellion that provides a pathway to greater growth and development. See illustration #6 on the following page.

**Illustration #6**. Female. Age 52. RH. Former nun. Left religious order in her early 40's. Her idealism and perfectionism couldn't tolerate the compromises the church required. Well organized, vital, active, goal oriented. The angularity shows her to be critical and demanding.

passed and so much

keep wondering about your for
me that I would have a destiny change.
It seems hard to believe that my life
could keep changing. I'm hoping it will
begin to settle in.
Included is a handwriting sample of
the man I have been seeing for about
3 months. His birthday is March 10 and he
will be 50 this year.

Anorexia is another example of the Good Girl syndrome and its consequences. Anorexia nervosa is a starvation behavior in which adolescent girls can go so far as to diet themselves out of existence in a sadly paradoxical attempt to gain control over their lives. It is thought that each year one in a hundred teenage girls chooses an emaciating anorexic regimen. According to Dr. Hilde Bruch, an authority on the problem, "Girls with conforming personalities feel obliged to do something that demands a great degree of independence in order to be respected and recognized.

When they get stuck, the only independence they feel they have is to control their bodies. The conviction of being inadequate is so deep seated and of such long standing that the girl withdraws behind the mask (read: persona) of superiority whenever she experiences the slightest self-doubt or encounters disagreement."

The very artificiality of the Persona means that a great deal of effort is used in its development and execution. Much time is taken in cultivating the details and outline of the mask to be worn. In addition to the affectation, it embodies there is also a strong element of compulsion. A significant amount of psychic energy is drained off in the effort to keep the mask in place.

That same energy is not available for use in other parts of the personality. It takes away from the richness of the inner life and the fullness of creative expression, shared reality, cultura l diversity, exploration of new dimensions of experience, and causes a diminishment of the interplay between the inner and outer reality. Often there is a high degree of achievement of certain kinds of goals based on living up to others' expectations and serious underachieving in living up to creative potentials. This form of compulsion works well as a defense against depression and many of the handwritings you are seeing are good examples of this dynamic. See illustrations #7 and #8 on the following pages. **Illustration #7**. Female. Age 35. RH. Accomplished crafts artist and teacher. Creative sophisticated forms. 'Good girl' facade and control lead to frustration and search for substitute emotional outlets. Balloon forms in lower zone are stuffed with repressed feelings of anger and guilt.

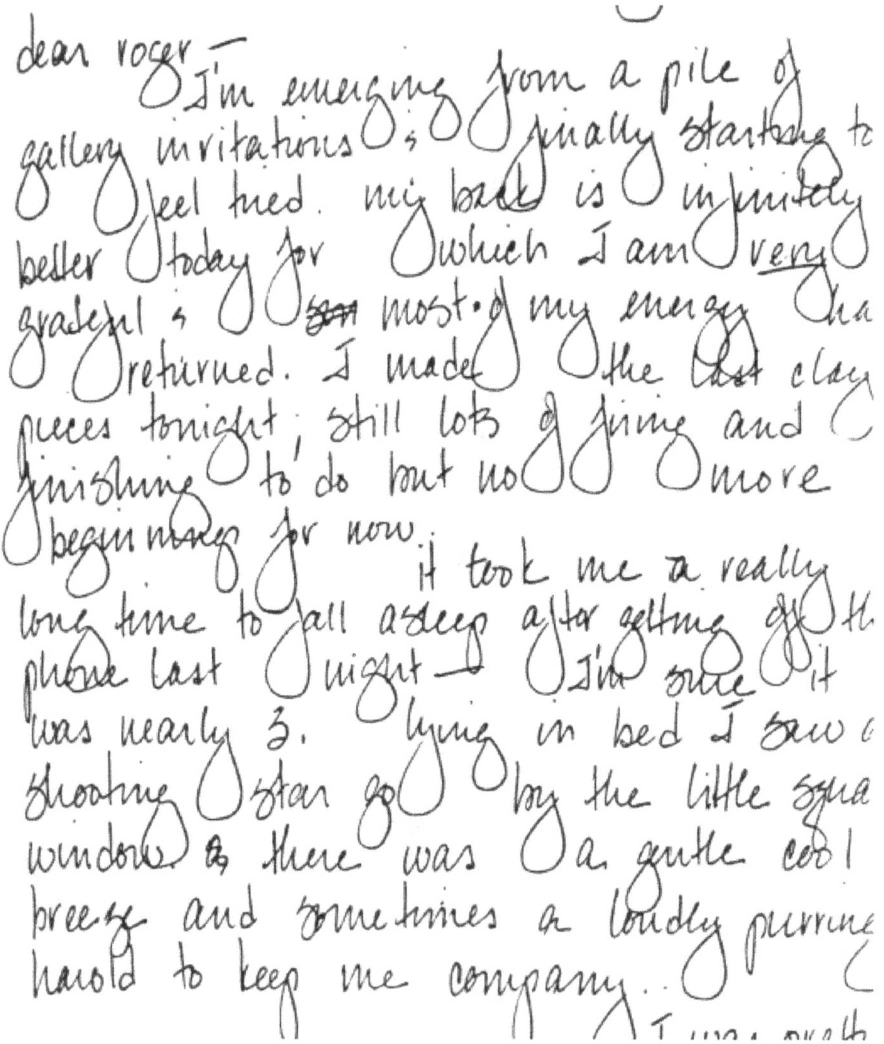
dear roger —
I'm emerging from a pile of
gallery invitations; finally starting to
feel tired. my back is infinitely
better today for which I am very
grateful; most of my energy has
returned. I made the last clay
pieces tonight; still lots of firing and
finishing to do but no more
beginnings for now.
it took me a really
long time to fall asleep after getting off the
phone last night — I'm sure it
was nearly 3. lying in bed I saw a
shooting star go by the little square
window & there was a gentle cool
breeze and sometimes a loudly purring
harold to keep me company.

**Illustration #8**. Female. Age 43. RH. This good girl kept sacrificing herself, first to family, then to husband, until she finally stood up for herself and got a Ph.D. in art education and left her husband. Weak ego strength is seen in uneven middle zone. Rounded forms and garlands show sensitivity and concern for others. Always doubts self-worth.

*The changes that have come since I last saw you have been many - and good. It was - and still is - a period of spiritual awakening. I took a leave from my job and went to Louisiana State Univ. for the year. Discovered how much truth you were on to regarding my love of teaching and learning. It was a great year!*

*I am here to look at the possibility of transferring to Columbia Teachers College - as the professor I want to study with at LSU has just accepted a position here. The decision to change is a hard one and I could return to LSU -*

*You said I'd be feeling uncertain come the end of the summer - and that the real change would come between ~~Sept.~~ July and October. I am trying to go with it - and am aware of a certain kind of harmony. [illegible] help with this*

In considering the persona it is important to remember that there are sane differences between men and women and their persona style. Dr. Lillian Rubin and others have written extensively about gender identity issues and the underlying motivations and fears that characterize the sexes. Girls are contending with the issue of bonding and merging with another and are powerfully motivated to sustain the unity of relationships. They will readily accept the demand to conform and subdue their impulses because their deepest fear is to be abandoned. In order to maintain the bond with another they will put up with more self-denial, and are therefore more ready to be "good."

This leads to looking nice, behaving in a more artificial manner, and wanting to have a likable appearance. All of which will show in handwriting very much the same way as forms that are less spontaneous, pretty in a contrived way, conforming to school type models, having a high degree of regularity and uniformity of forms, and diminished creativity.

Boys deal with the issue of maintaining and sustaining their separateness and apartness. they are afraid of losing their identity through merging with another. What troubles them is fear of helplessness, submission to another, and loss of strength, a strength which can only be maintained by their separateness.

Psychoanalytically, it would be associated with the castration anxiety. Boys and, later, men act in a more demanding and dominating manner, making others submit and conform to them and their desires. The male persona is represented by the attitude of "machismo," a projected image of. power, potency, virility, and honor. It represents apartness, territoriality, uncompromising insistence on a code of behavior, and a willingness to fight. In handwriting it is seen often as an emphasis on angularity, heavy pressure, large initial letters, sudden changes in direction, and a lack of roundedness.

Another of the Persona types is associated with what Dr. David Shapiro calls the "Hysterical Style." This is an intense need for love and admiration, a concern with external appearance and the amount of attention received from others, all of which creates an aura of egocentricity. Superficial warmth, intense emotionality and self-dramatization characterize a very expressive style of behavior.

The hysteric uses intensity of feeling and seductiveness to protect against the real experience of deep feelings, especially sexual feelings. The hysteric style is one of transience and impressionability with little reference to inner realities and a general lack of self-understanding. In handwriting this Persona is characterized by overdone forms with exaggerated movements or elaborations, poor and confused space picture, inconsistent simplification. See illustration #9.

**Illustration #9**. Female. Early thirties. RH. Successful and high-powered publicist. Example of hysterical style. Makes strong impression but is very confused as to her real inner identity. She uses activity, emotivity and distraction to keep deeper feelings away from consciousness.

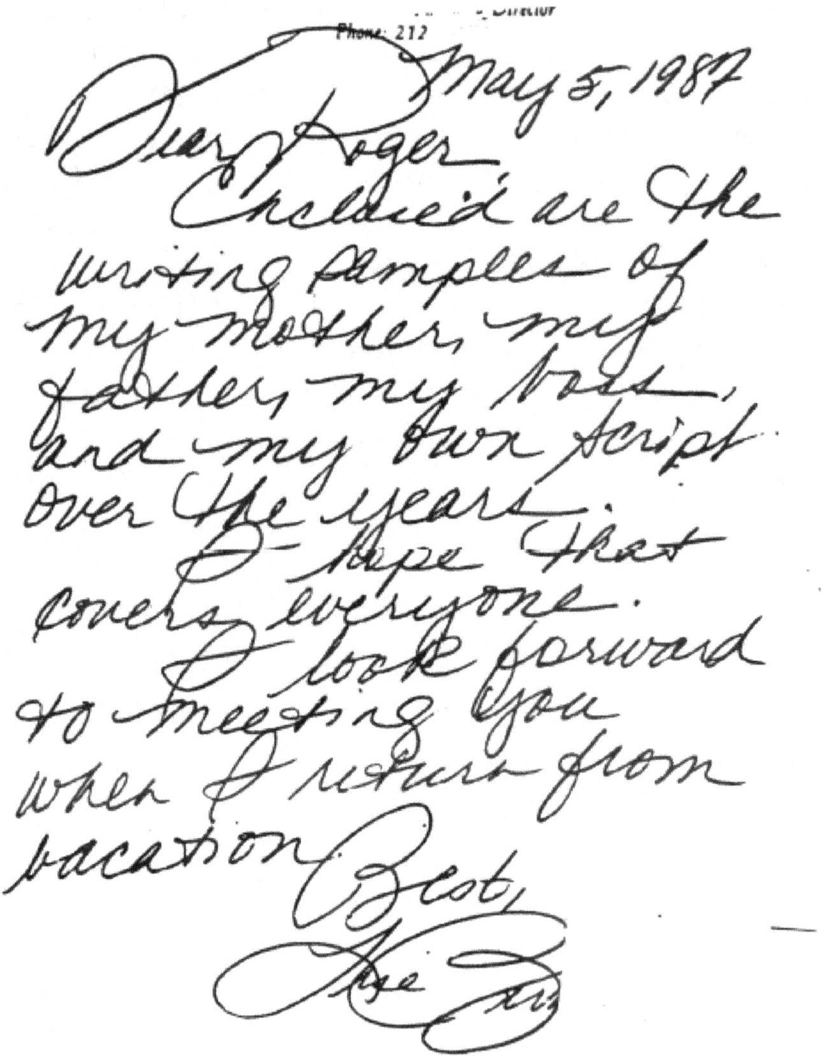

Director
Phone: 212

May 5, 1987

Dear Roger
Enclosed are the writing samples of my mother, my father, my boss, and my own script over the years.
I hope that covers everyone.
I look forward to meeting you when I return from vacation.
Best,

Calligraphy, when it is used as one's normal, everyday writing style, represents a form of facade writing, an aesthetic persona. Calligraphic writing is disconnected and therefore slower than cursive. Because it is to some extent flourished and elaborated in the execution of these separate forms, it is highly self-conscious writing style.

It is drawn rather than spontaneous, contrived rather than natural, enriched rather than simplified. Attention is drawn to the way things look, so that one can see that the writer's consciousness is very involved with the appearances and the impression being made on the viewer.

Calligraphy can be analyzed using standard graphological principles but it requires skill and experience. A good starting point would be an examination of Chinese and Japanese calligraphers. There one can see the clear expression of individuality within a strict stylistic tradition.

The signature is often the part of the handwriting that is used to express the writer's persona image, the way he wants to be thought of by others. It is the most public part of one's writing and is used as the singular identifying mark and authentication for all legal and financial transactions.

If the Persona is one of modesty the signature will be smaller than the body of writing. The need to enlarge the public image is seen in a signature larger than regular script or with very enlarged capital letters. Paraphs or underlining provides bolstering to the ego image. A first name made larger than the last emphasized indicates the importance of personal achievements or a diminution of family influence.

## BIBLIOGRAPHY


Bruch, Hilde, M.D. Eating Disorders, New York: Basic Books, 1973.

Dowling, Colette. 'The Cinderella Complex, New York: Simon & Schuster Pocket Books 1981.

Jacobi, Jolande. The Psychology of C.G. Jung, Yale University Press, 1973.

Progoff, Ira. Jung's Psychology and Its Social Meaning, New York: Dialogue House Library, 1953.

Rubin, Lillian. Intimate Strangers, New York: Harper & Row, 1984.

Shapiro, David. Neurotic Styles, New York: Basic Books, 1965.

Winnicott, D.W. Home is Where We Start From, New York: W.W. Norton, 1986.

# Aspects of Anger and Aggression In Handwriting Analysis

# Aspects of Anger and Aggression

In order to have some grasp of the uses and meanings of anger it is important to appreciate its role as part of the human survival response. Anger and fear are the two basic emotions that motivate our behavior in times of stress and emergency. They are built into us to help alert us to the presence of danger and to prepare us to meet that challenge through the "fight or flight" mechanism. These emotions trigger a series of involuntary responses through the autonomic nervous system.

Pupils dilate or constrict. Palms become sweaty. Adrenaline is pumped into the blood altering heart rate and breathing, and blood is redirected to different parts of the body, certain muscles are contracted and opposing ones relaxed, just to name a few of the many changes that occur.

We also experience the feeling of the emotion—fear or rage or both at once. In our earlier, primitive, pre-civilized condition the fear response could become contagious and alert our group to a common danger. In addition, the fear or anger signals would be sensed by the attacker, especially if it was another human being, and alert him to our willingness to run, or stand and defend our turf. These emergency emotions give notice of intentions so that anger can be used to avoid conflict as well as to resolve it.

That in brief form is the Darwinian concept which associates us with other higher animal forms in the use of the fear and anger response to insure both individual and species survival. But in today's highly civilized world seldom, if ever, do we experience a direct threat to our physical existence.

We are most likely to feel fear or anger when we sense disapproval, deprivation, exploitation and manipulation, frustration, betrayal, or humiliation. We have come to experience these affronts as if they were threats to survival. These are the assaults that threaten our security and arouse anger, and they are not simple. They produce clusters of feeling rather than a single emotion which reflects the complexity of the problem and of our lives: hurt and jealousy, rage and fear, sadness and desire, joy, and guilt.

How does the anger/fear response develop in the human psyche? The psychiatrist, John Bowlby, believes that the infant directly relates the relief of pain and distress with its scream, as if the scream were directly converted into food or comfort. In a few short months the infant begins to differentiate himself from his environment and realizes he is not omnipotent. The fact of life that he faces is that he is a totally helpless creature only able to survive with the assistance of others. When his needs are met by caring parents security prevails, but there is an ever present danger. What if the parents disappear? What if they stop caring and withdraw their love? This is the great threat of early life: separation, abandonment, and isolation. (Ill.# 2)

**ILLUSTRATION #1**. Male. Age 33. Wide spaces show early abandonment, emotional isolation, and detachment. He is a drug abuser, as well as homosexual and has attempted suicide. He works as a makeup artist, but is often not very functional.

Today when I woke I had
a sore throat. I went to my
doctor at 12:30. He told me
I had a sore throat and to
take the pills he prescribed.

**ILLUSTRATION #2.** Female. Age 37. In foster homes for first six years. Lived with severely disturbed mother and abusive father from age 6 to 16. Is quite intelligent and wants to be a writer. Often feels psychologically unbalanced and is subject to sudden rages. Notice the unexpected stops and changes of direction.

Dear Roger
A Very lost soul who studies
African dance wonders if you are not
a human computer, and being
most tired, doesn't know how or
what to write. I only wanted
on you once.
Tix

**ILLUSTRATION #3.** Female. Age 12. Sexually abused between ages 7 to 11 by uncle who is now in jail. Strong indications of emotional damage with identity problems and unstable mood swings. She is one of five siblings experiencing different levels of abuse.

"The date is Tomorrow!" ILL.4
yelled Mrs. Sleepy
In the morning the
door bell rang it was
a figure. Not really a man or
woman because it was white
and had long hair.
"I am your daughters
guardian angle" said
the figure.
"Why are you Here?"
asked mrs. Sleepy.
"I am Here to see she gets
a good Home." said the figure
"Will you feed it and close it?"
asked the figure again

**ILLUSTRATION #4**. Female. Age 25. Rigid upbringing and severe, disapproving parents. Pent up frustration and anger with no release. Needs antidepressants to keep functioning.

Dear Rodger,

Here is my "dear Rodger" letter. Enclosed is a sample of my handwriting from the past as well as a sample of my mothers handwriting. I think it should probably be enough of a sample for you to get whatever information you need from it.

The first response to separation is fear followed quickly by rage. The fear of abandonment survives into adulthood, often in disguised and complicated forms. We will rage at any suggestion of neglect from those we love and on whom we depend. Whenever separation is temporary, which it usually is, anger has two functions according to Bowlby. First "it may assist in overcoming such obstacles as there may be to reunion; second, it may discourage the loved person from going away again."

He also notes that children can develop an anger of despair when they are subjected to repeated, prolonged separations, or when they are constantly threatened with abandonment. They then feel enraged at the person who inflicts such intense pain of loss. This same anger of despair can result from having abusive parents. If the parent or loved one never returns despair turns into detachment or listlessness. This sequence from protest to despair to detachment will follow the child into adulthood as a reaction to separation. (Il. #1, #3)

Of the experiences that make us feel threatened, disapproval is one of the most powerful. In the training of children, the granting or withholding of approval is a most potent tool. There are also many forms of direct disapproval or punishment used for training or guidance. Our power to survive as children is very limited and it is very important that the parenting figures love and approve of us. Otherwise, we will feel weak and unable to manage without the services of those powerful others. So, the most dangerous thing in the world is not to be loved by them.

All of us enter adult life with a sense of vulnerability which makes us feel threatened when someone of importance withdraws love from us or when some other imperils that love. Withdrawal of love puts our sense of. self-esteem and worth into question, and that diminution of power can trigger hurt and angry reactions. The more dependent a person is, the more he needs reassurance. At the extreme of insecurity, any criticism is felt as a threat. Merely raising questions about lovability or worth can create stress, including either a frightened or angry response. Willard Gaylin, whose work is referred to and paraphrased extensively in this brief study, states that "sensitivity to approval and disapproval is always at its most intense in loving situations. It is not surprising that most of us reserve most of our anger for those we love." (Ill. #2 #4 # 5)

**ILLUSTRATION #5**. Female. Age 57. Worked hard and fruitlessly to win over emotionally unavailable parents and rejecting husband. Escaped into fantasies & aesthetics. Underachieving & immature.

am I going to Roger;
because you too long
I have not known
this machine, this
human calculator, this
spirit, this body, this
organism.
And why have I
with much energy and time
done others? I think
for many reasons
and all have the same.

Betrayal is another anger generator. When those we depend on for love and support betray that trust, we feel outraged and hurt. Abandonment by a source of love is a signal of worthlessness. The betrayed person feels unloved, unsure, and used. The trusted one is revealed as the enemy and this is compounded by rage with one's self for having allowed the deception. Betrayal can cause an explosive upsurge of anger, especially if sexuality is involved. Attacking the sense of sexual worth strikes at the core of male and female security. Such betrayals

The feeling of deprivation breeds resentment and anger. But it can only be understood in a relative sense. For instance, one can be surrounded by riches and affluence and feel deprived, or one can endure severe poverty where everything is measured and rationed and still not feel deprived. Gaylin says, "deprivation emerges from a sense of what one has in terms of what one thinks others have. It suggests that somehow or other that which is rightly yours has not been given you—or worse—has been taken from you.

What is rightly yours is usually measured in terms of that which others receive." This is often the basis of rivalry and competition in childhood, and underlies many sibling conflicts. If what we do is not acknowledged or rewarded fairly or equitably, the anger and resentment that develops will be directed at those who are depriving us and later be extended, often unreasonably, to those getting more than we are in the same situation. It is important to remember that we cannot afford to sustain our anger for too long to those in power, so we displace it elsewhere, to friends, neighbors, family, or colleagues. (Il. 6)

**ILLUSTRATION #6.** Female. Age 39. Parents demanding and critical. She always felt shortchanged in struggles with brother. Although driven, success and recognition eluded her. Often depressed & angry.

Dear Roger:

[illegible]

Gaylin comments further about social inequity: "It is not just one authority but all authority that is at fault. When the deprivation can be associated with station, gender, race or class, the social order will be viewed as the unfair agent and unfairness will be relabeled injustice. Alienation is almost always a product of the resentment that comes from living in a society perceived as unjust. Acts against the social order are viewed differently when the social order is seen as supporting an immoral state of affairs." (Ill. #8)

If, in addition to the perception of social injustices, a child is truly deprived because of illegitimacy, a broken home or alcoholic or otherwise abusive parenting, he may be damaged beyond hope of repair. His psychological injuries and anger will make him feel cheated in the midst of abundance and good fortune. There is a core group of people in our society whose rage is barely hidden, whose behaviors are largely antisocial and who are likely to remain unredeemable and threatening.

Humiliation is another cause of anger. It is the ultimate form of degradation. When the fact is exposed that we are less than lovable, less than potent, and when those inadequacies are revealed to the public eye and knowledge we experience a devaluation of the most painful order. To be reduced as an individual in our own eyes is hard enough to bear, but to be shamed openly, before a group, decreases our worth and adds immeasurable pain. This can convert anger into outrage and hurt into wrath and breech our normal restraints. (Ill.# 7)

**ILLUSTRATION #7**. Male. Age 43. Toilet trained at 12 months. Uses tension and angry feelings to achieve success in finance. Any hint of failure brings on feelings of shame and humiliation.

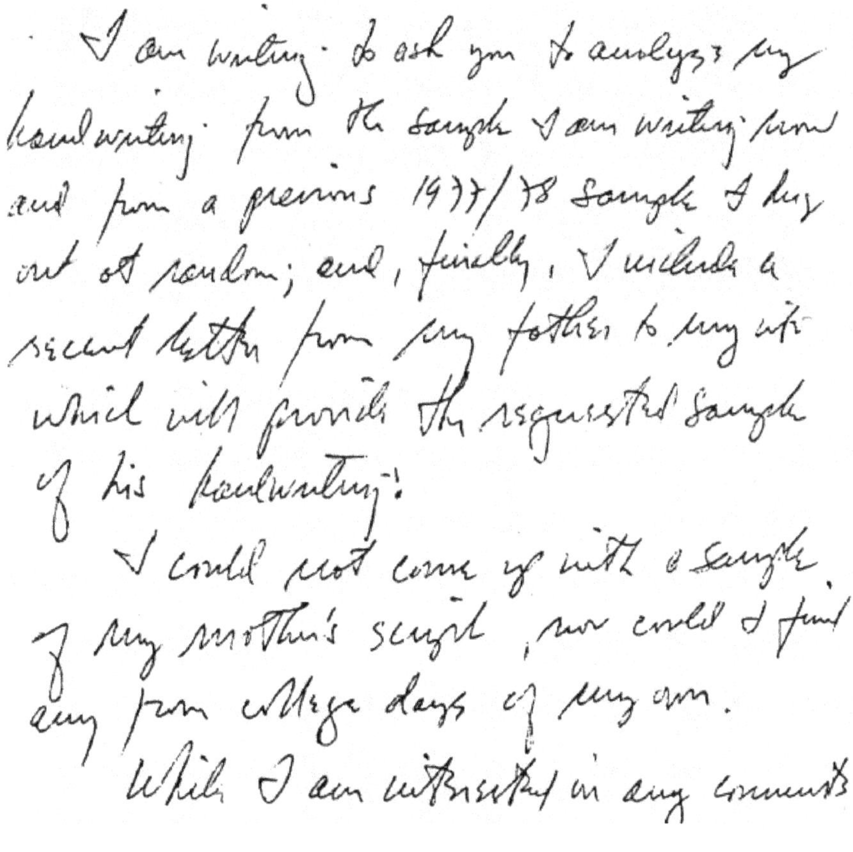

I am writing to ask you to analyze my handwriting from the sample I am writing now and from a previous 1977/78 sample I dug out at random; and, finally, I include a recent letter from my father to my wife which will provide the requested sample of his handwriting.

I could not come up with a sample of my mother's script, nor could I find any from college days of my own.

While I am interested in any comments

**ILLUSTRATION #8.** Male. Age 33. Upper class South American belonged to revolutionary group to fight and undermine the current system. Intelligence and rigidity underlie strict ideology. Writing is tense with cut off movements showing aggression.

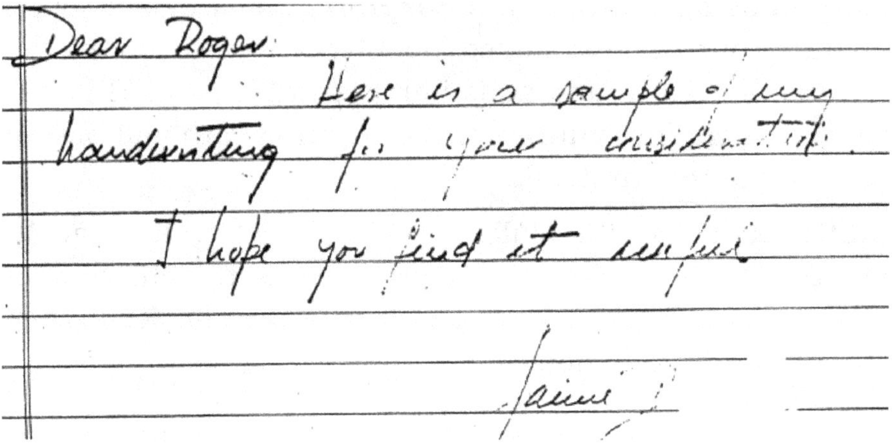

Dear Roger:
Here is a sample of my handwriting for your consideration.
I hope you find it useful.
Jaime

**ILLUSTRATION #9.** Female. Age 38. Bitter at injustices of past, especially toward family. Acts passive aggressively by talking without end, not allowing the listener to escape, and an innocent oblivion to the listener's reaction. Very crowded space, excessive circularity and elaborations show poor judgment & self-involvement.

Dear Roger,

It's been a rather hectic day. Painters, workmen, delivery people etc. I had planned to send off this sample of my writing this afternoon, but forgot. Hope this arrives by Saturday as a friend shall be mailing this tonight.

I must say, that it was rather strange to speak to someone for the first time & give so much personal data.

A friend came for dinner tonight. Rather hysterical evening. She is about 4 inches taller than I & trying on some of my clothes was a great sketch for T.V.

Hope this is the writing sample you wanted.

**ILLUSTRATION # 10.** Male. No Age. Homosexual. Rejected by mother at birth. Contracted AIDS deliberately to get back at her. She had to take care of him during the last year of his life.

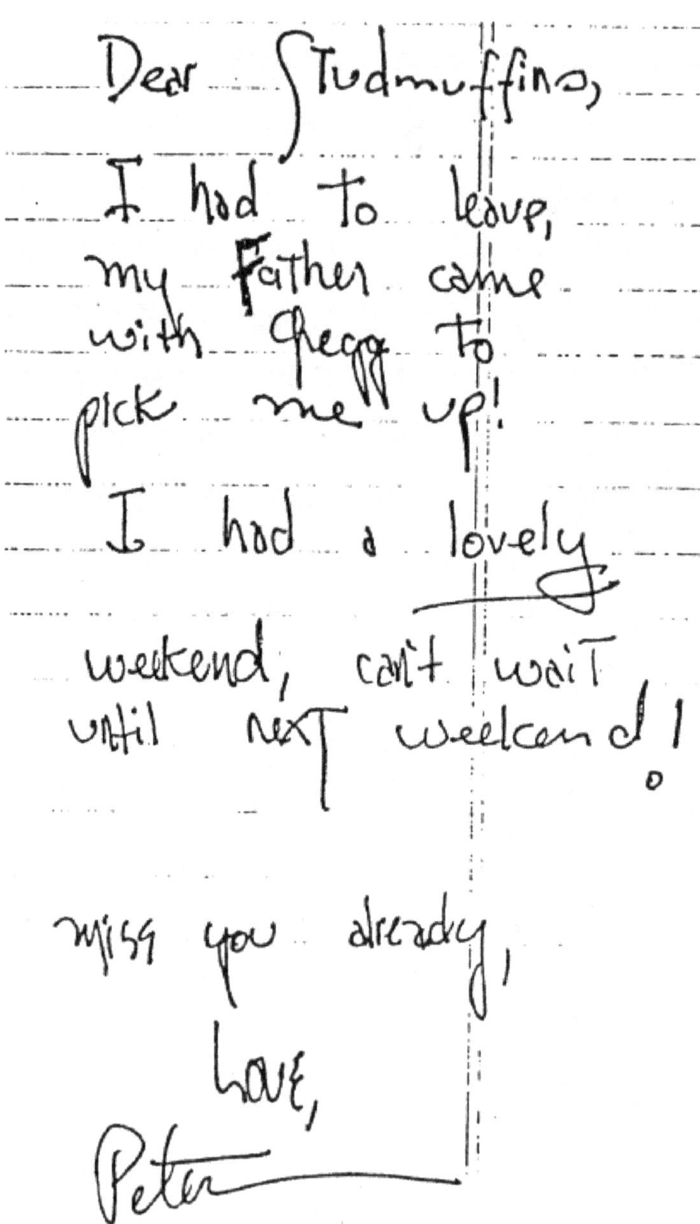
Dear Studmuffins,
I had to leave,
my Father came
with Gregg to
pick me up!
I had a lovely
weekend, can't wait
until next weekend!
miss you already,
Love,
Peter

**ILLUSTRATION #11**. Female. Age 38. Adopted age 1. Brought up by guilt-dispensing adoptive mother. Writer felt anger toward mother and sister, below, but denied it and appeased them instead. 'Good girl' syndrome. Allows herself to be taken advantage of by others out of fear of rejection.

I am enclosing the handwriting<br>
of two women - Rose Slivka who I<br>
work with at Craft International and<br>
Margaret Richardson who I may<br>
be working with on a new magazine<br>
I am looking forward to seeing<br>
you on the 30th. I'm eager to<br>
hear your comments on these two<br>
ladies.

**ILLUSTRATION #12**. Female. Age 40. Adoptive sister of ill #11. Needy, demanding and angry. Always felt threatened by sister and asked for, and received more. Not very functional. Emotionally and intellectually undeveloped. Tight, tense, rigid writing with strong left slant shows inability to release feelings or grudges.

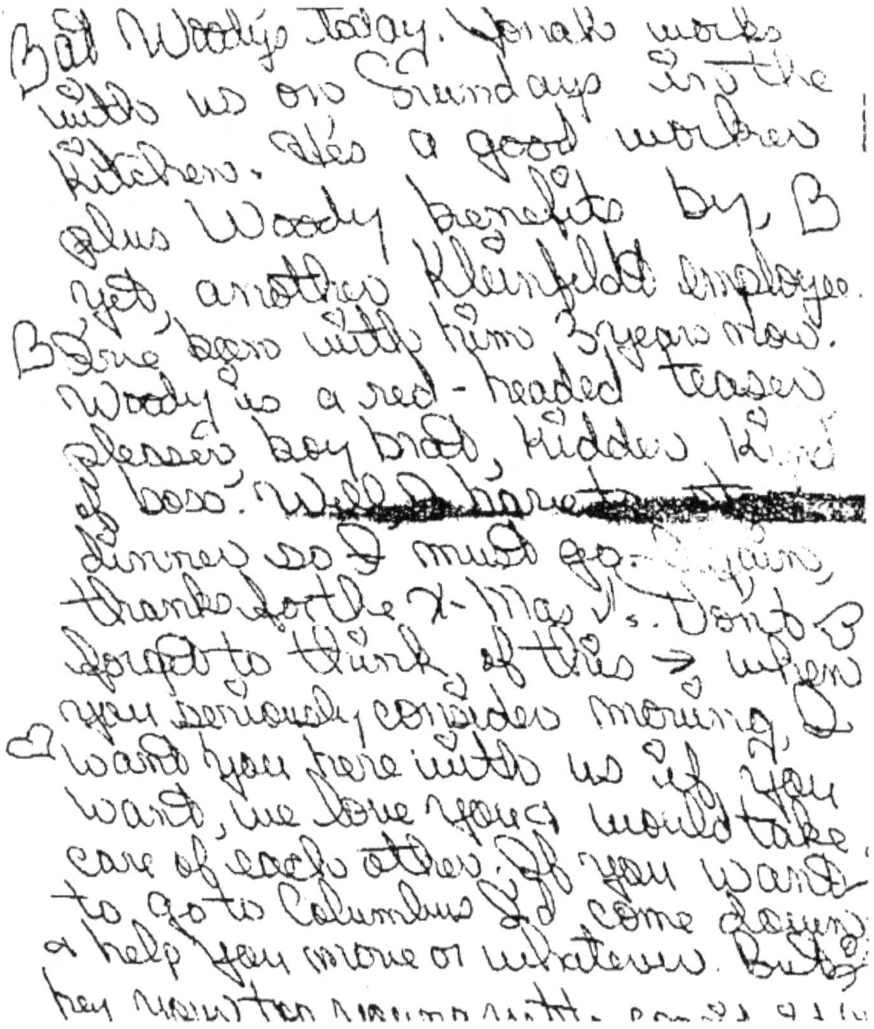

**ILLUSTRATION #13.** Male. Age late 40's. Pious and devoted to his religious beliefs, erupted out of denial, and killed his wife, children, and mother-in-law 'to protect their souls from damnation.' Assumed another identity and lived in peaceful denial for 21 more uneventful years until apprehended and tried for murder.

One other thing. It may seem cowardly to have always shot from behind but I didn't want any of them to know even at the last second that I had to do this to them.

John got shot more because he seemed to struggle longer. The rest were immediately out of the pain. John ~~probably~~ didn't consciously feel anything either.

Please remember me in your prayers. I will need them whether or not the government does its duty as it see it. I'm only concerned with making my peace with God + of this I am assured because of Christ dying even for me.

P.S. Mother is in the hallway in the attic - 3rd floor. She was too heavy to move.

John.

Frustration causes tension which can move easily into the emotion of anger. It is caused by the blocking of a goal and anyone experiencing frustration when attempting even minor tasks is aware of how quickly their irritability level can be elevated and anger-produced. Some of us have learned to cope well when things don't go their way, and others have a very low tolerance level for that challenge. Frustration triggers a sense of impotence because a large or small problem can't be solved. The annoyance and anger that arises is often deflected to others. It is here that spouses children and others that will not strike back become very handy to have around. (Ill. #12 & #14)

Gaylin refers to research where "it was found that a number of experimental psychological and sociological conditions could increase the probability or ferocity of anger. The most effective included frustration, an increase of sexual arousal, hunger, and fatigue. Others included isolation, overcrowding and the disruption of a steady metabolic state such as sleep or meditation." Add noise to that list, as well.

Being human gives us the capacity to anticipate and predict. This means we have the ability to use other emotions for checking anger and buying time. for more complicated forms of defense or aggression. Vengeance, retaliation, vendettas, and the spinning of plots, often associated with injured pride or ambition, require a clear head and planned, unemotional aggressiveness. That is the difference between hostile aggression motivated by anger, and instrumental aggression, which is the elimination of an obstacle standing between an aggressor and a goal, when such behavior is not motivated by angry feelings. (Ill. #8 & #13)

**ILLUSTRATION #14.** Female. Age 40. Successful graphics designer. Is narcissistic, impatient, and impulsive. Has low tolerance for frustration. She is extremely sensitive to slights and has a quick irritability trigger. Needs to work with easy going, low key associates that can tolerate her flare ups.

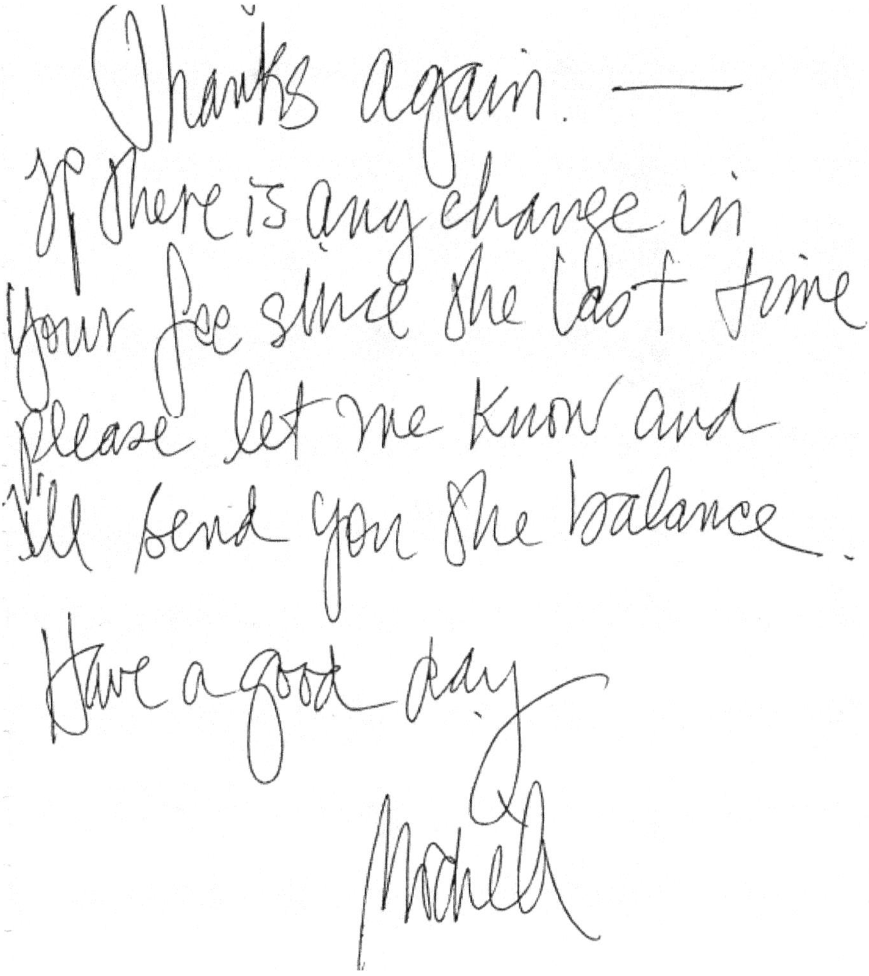

Thanks again. —
If there is any change in
your fee since the last time
please let me know and
I'll send you the balance.

Have a good day
Michele

**ILLUSTRATION #15.** Male. Age 22. Highly insecure with serious identity problems. Although intelligent, he is underdeveloped and underachieving. Lives emotionally isolated from others and is often severely depressed, once to the point of attempting suicide with a 12 inch knife.

My life has been characterized by a unfortunate feeling that I have yet to maximize my real potential and utilize my true energies which I are stored within. This is manifested in my inability to stay in school and a reluctance to work or more simply to be active. I now think of myself as being lazy. Unable to carrythrough with a goal or project.

I am an only child. I stay by myself most

**ILLUSTRATION #16.** Hale. Age 19. Left-handed. Large distance between words, a wandering baseline, a downward slant and poorly executed, neglected forms indicate strong depressive tendencies. His parents were not available emotionally. His introversion and withdrawal hide his bottled up anger.

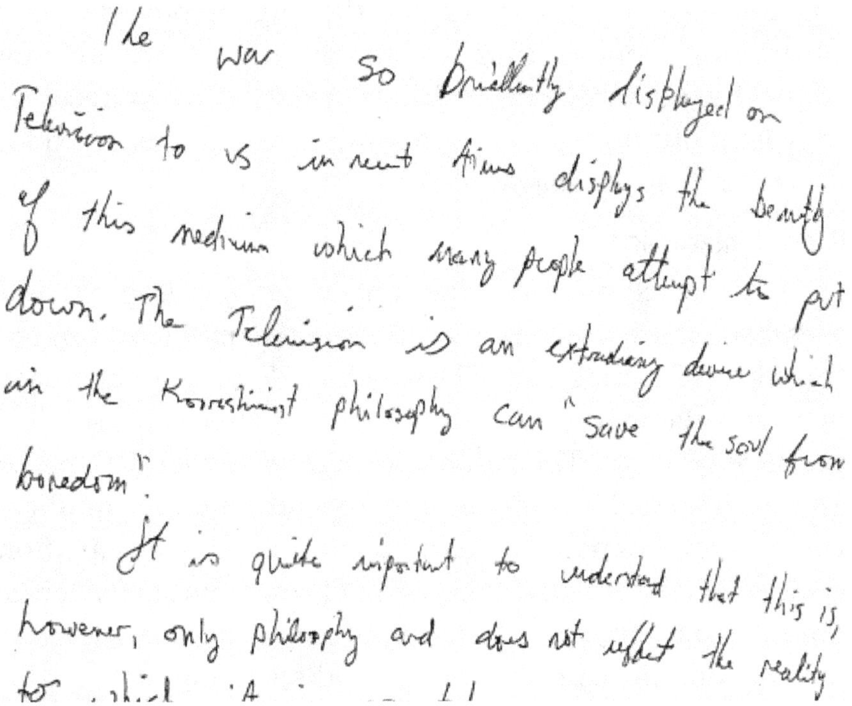

The war so brilliantly displayed on Television to us in recent times displays the beauty of this medium which many people attempt to put down. The Television is an extraordinary device which in the Korrestinist philosophy can "save the soul from boredom".

It is quite important to understand that this is, however, only philosophy and does not reflect the reality for which

There are a number of ways to handle anger. Guilt is a very effective one. When rage is directed inappropriately we are likely to experience a painful sense of guilt which can then check the rage or limit it. When guilt is absent as a restraint it allows for child abuse, wife beating, sadism and antisocial behavior. It is also a powerful component in the "good child" syndrome. Denial is another mechanism for control. It means that you hide the anger from yourself by controlling feelings that are too frightening to acknowledge. One acts as if anger doesn't exist for them because if they let it out it might turn into murderous rage. Therefore, it is utterly suppressed. (ill.11&13)

**Passive-aggression**

Another commonly experienced defense is passive aggression. It's a convenient device for expressing anger in the form of a disguise. Those who are passive aggressive deceive themselves into thinking that they harbor no aggressive feelings. Their behavior can easily be rationalized as non-aggressive and there is a vague, indirect quality to their angry feelings that can't be attack ed frontally. Some typical behaviors are sarcasm, chronic lateness for appointments, emotional detachment, sexual withdrawal, psychosomatic complaints, guilt dispensing, martyrdom, stubbornness, and others.

The following illustrations are typical of passive aggression. A man puts a new lock on the front door and forgets to give his wife the key, or he talks on the phone for an hour when he knows his girlfriend is trying to call. (ill. #9 & #10)

Scapegoating or bigotry is yet another defense against rage. It needs an object of hate onto which can be projected frustration, anger, and feelings of impotence. It is another variation on the use of project ion as a device for dissipating anger and self-hatred. Scapegoating allows us to find someone other than ourselves to blame for our misery. It protects the bigots damaged self-image and fragile self- respect.

Carol Tavris, in *Anger, The Misunderstood Emotion,* has an interesting discussion of anger and depression. In 1911 Karl Abraham hypothesized that hostility about the loss of a loved one becomes self-directed, and this process leads to depression. Freud, in Mourning and Melancholia, added that guilt over a loss produces a need to suffer which triggers self-directed hostility.

Most psychoanalytic writers subsequently put aggression or anger at the center of their theories of depression. Gaylin writes that in clinical situations "the stimulation of anger, even artificially, has a salutary, if temporary, influence on a depressed patient. Closely related to this is the fact that excessive compassion, sympathy, pity, or commiseration on the part of others will often drive a depressed patient to suicide. Within the profession, this has come to be known as "killing with kindness."

Suicidc is most often accompanied by severe depression and it can be considered an acting out of impounded rage directed against the self. There has been much research on the connect ion between anger and depression since Freud, and the findings about anger as a primary cause of depression have been called into question. The development of anti-depressant drugs, for example, is hard to explain and incorporate into the psychoanalytic theory of depression. "Nonetheless," says Gaylin, "the fixed relationship between the impounding of anger and the feeling of depression is an empiric fact that will not go away." (ill. #15 & #16)

There is a relationship between the emotions and physical disorders. Those that are most commonly considered psychosomatic are hypertension, hives, eczema asthma, glaucoma, duodenal ulcer, myocardial infarction. Whether anger can be pinpointed as the major cause of certain conditions, as separated from fear or guilt, is not clear. What is clear is that a group of powerful emotions in which anger is a central force is a major factor in these psychosomatic conditions. Repressed anger can do damage.

## Graphological indicators of anger and aggression

The "fight or flight" response is incorporated into each and every one of us, either through genetics, the environment, or a combination of both. That means we all possess the capacity for, and the experience of anger, fear, and, at least to some extent, aggression. Therefore, in every handwriting the capacity for anger should be evident. But, because it is often mixed with or diffused by other graphic expressions of emotion, or psychological indicators, the graphic signs of anger/aggression are not always easy to pinpoint in every script.

The following shows some of the indicators that give a clearer signal and should be looked for by the graphologist. They will reveal, in varying degrees, the tension, anxiety and irritability that underlie anger and aggressiveness.

**ALL EXTREMES** reveal anxiety and poor emotional integration often associated with anger or inappropriate emotional expression.

**ANGLES** show a readiness for friction and action, except in the script of older writers.

**CLUB STROKES** increase size and pressure at end of stroke and show a capacity to impose will or strike out at object.

**EXCESSIVE PRESSURE** shows friction, tension and bottled up frustration, inflexibility, and unwillingness to adjust.

**EXCESS CIRCULARITY** reveals a buildup of emotional needs that can result in a volatile emotional discharge.

**LARGE WRITING** shows pride, often with doubtful self-esteem, making writer sensitive to any criticism (seen as humiliation).

**LARGE SPACES BETWEEN WORDS AND/OR NEGLECT OF FORM** can show

reduced empathy and willingness to live by one's own rules. Often easily offended, with heightened irritability.

**LETTERS GETTING LARGER AT END OF WORD** show stubbornness, self-assertiveness, and readiness to resist.

**MIXED SLANT** can express anxiety, sensitivity, and irritability.

**NARROWNESS** means less release, more tension and frustration.

**RIGIDITY & RIGID REGULARITY** shows frustration, held in anger, tension, harsh judgments, potential for unemotional aggression.

**SLACK WRITING** shows impulsiveness, unpredictability, and outbursts of temper due to irritability.

**SUDDEN STOPS OR CHANGES OF DIRECTION** is one of the strongest indicators for irritability, anger, and aggressive eruptions.

**T CROSS SLANTED DOWN** especially with pressure shows a desire to impose one's will on others

**UNEVEN PRESSURE** shows variable energy and unpredictable bursts of activity or passivity, with higher sensitivity and irritability.

**UNEVEN SPACE BETWEEN LETTERS** means uneven emotional release patterns causing sudden flareups, anxiety and irritability.

**VARIABLE BASELINE** means high sensitivity and strong mood swings with potential for angry or aggressive behavior.

## BIBLIOGRAPHY

Bowlby, John. *Attachment and Loss*, vol.2. New York. Basic Books, 1973

Bychowski, Gustav. *Patterns of Anger* in Psychoanalytic Study of The Child, Vol 21, pp. 172 - 191. New York: International Universities Press, 1966

Gaylin, Willard. *The Rage Within: Anger in Modern Life*. New York. Penguin Books, 1984

Gaylin, Willard. *Feelings: Our Vital Signs*. New York: Harper & Row, 1979

Grunwald, Lisa. *The Passive Aggressive Male.*" Esquire. pp. 105 - 115. April, 1989

Roman, Klara. *Handwriting: A Key To Personality*. New York: Pantheon Books, 1952

Speilberger, C.D.

Jacobs, G.

Russell. S.

Crane, R.S. *Assessment Of Anger* in *Advances in Personality Assessment*, Vol. 2, pp. 161-1889 Hillsdale, NJ: Lawrence Erlbaum Assoc.

Tavris, Carol. Anger: *The Misunderstood Emotion*. New York: Simon & Schuster, 1989

# Identifying the Mother and Father in Handwriting

# Identifying the mother and father in handwriting

The parents, to the extent that they exist in the handwriting, exist only on a symbolic basis. A symbol being a graphic impulse or expression that stands in, so to speak, for the real object; and the way one treats this symbolic expression reveals the attitudes and feelings toward that person or thing.

The handwriting analyst can say from these symbolic expressions that a certain kind of event or experience in the life of an individual could have produced that particular symbolic response. In handwriting one sees the psychological result and, perhaps, the psychological event, but never the actual person that is being symbolized. The analyst is two times removed from the facts. One cannot judge. the parents themselves as personalities unless their script is available. It should be understood that any judgment regarding the parents' influence should be confirmed by at least three indicators in the script.

The formation of the personality proceeds in progressive stages. If development is arrested at one stage it will. inhibit the normal growth pattern and prevent the proper completion of other stages. As Dr. Dettweiler has pointed out in *Jugend in Not* it is of critical importance that the infant, between the sixth month and the 24th month, make the initial "dual union" with the mother. This is the primary connection to another human being and is undoubtedly the single most important phase in personality development. Here the infant feels accepted, loved, his needs satisfied, and is psychologically united with another being.

He is able to merge his being with another safely, securely, and joyfully. The next step is developing the triangular connection between mother, father, and child. This necessitates a loosening of the mother-child bond and begins the relationship to the father, the family organization, and the larger world. Now the child be gins to establish his own identity. This takes place right after the dual union. The next major phase of development is in late pre-puberty or early puberty when the child develops his social and group identity.

**If the child did not make the union with the mother the other stages cannot develop properly.**

Dr. Bernhard Wittlich in his description of the neurotic character feels that this period of development and its attendant problems with the mother is the source of the schizoid or depressive character structures. As the proper relationship to the nether determines whether a connection can be made to the father at all—so a proper connection to the father determines whether a healthy social identity can be formed.

According to Dr. Dettweiler, the graphic indicators that show disturbances in the dual union and the resulting emotional isolation are found in letters that are split within themselves or done with two separate writing impulses, such as in "d," "a," "g," or "k"; or in letters that should touch the base line but do not, such as in the letter "h" (ill. #1); or in extreme distance between words; or excessive circularity.

I thought this chart might

Because the relationship to the parents is such a profound formative influence on the personality, and the influence colors, limits, defines, and pervades so much of the psyche, the parents will have an immeasurably important effect upon the handwriting. Their traces will be found throughout the script.

There is no part of the writing that does not show the symbolic presence of the parents. There are, however, areas in the writing that have a stronger symbolic meaning for either the mother or the father. These are associated with the various psychosocial functions relating to them. The upper zone and right side—the father. The lover zone and the left side—the mother.

### Left And Right And The Parents

Of the two fundamental directions in handwriting, horizontal and vertical movement, the horizontal movement from left to right is the primary. The point at which we begin to write—the left side—stands for the past, the beginning, the source, the origin, the initial coming into being, and naturally, the mother. All movement begins with the purpose of moving rightward even though it may not start in a rightward direction.

This is the inner drive towards the outer reality, the world around us, the future—as it implies action to be completed, purpose, orientation away from the self and also the father. The father principle within us is how we feel about actualizing ourselves in the cosmos. (ill. #2)

my embalmer has allowed me to use
(see enclosed card) and I plan to

**TREND**

Since most writing involves movement both to the left and right, right trend is seen when the rightward direction is stronger than the left. The failure to move rightward where it is efficient and to be expected is, by definition, left trend. Right trend shows good adjustment to the father, the father principle, and the acceptance of his model. (ill. #3)

not to try too much before
be forced to do it.

Left trend shows avoidance or conflict with the father figure, and a turning back toward the mother image out of insecurity, fear, or a preference for that parent or the inner self. Trend is most easily seen in the upper zone or lower zone. It is in the lower zone, particularly, where the unconscious attitudes toward the parents are so vividly expressed.

Left trend in the lower zone shows preference for the mother over the father, (ill. #4) or unresolved problems with the mother that must be overcome before the proper father orientation can be established.

visiting a few art galleries

**Right trend in the lower zone shows instinctual harmony and adjustment to both mother and father.**

Right trend in the upper zone shows good adaptation to the values and ideals of the father. Left trend here shows either a conflict with the father's values or the preference for values from another source. Trend in the middle zone, although seen in many ways, shows most clearly in the word endings.

Right trend shows a harmony and confidence that the father will be supportive of one's ego and emotional needs. Left trend indicates disappointment, suspicion, and fearfulness of the father's response to the ego and emotional requirements. An example of contradiction in the trend would be seen in a strong right movement within a word that ends in a leftward direction. This would symbolize a strong desire to reach out to the father, but also the persistent pattern of rejection or avoidance, which would generate insecurity and ambivalence toward him. (ill. #5)

### Vertical Movement And The Parents

The primary vertical movement is the downstroke. It is the reverse in meaning of the horizontal movement. It begins away from the writer and ends closer to him. It takes outside influences and carries them within. Symbolically, it begins in the realm of the father and ends in the realm of the mother, moving from the superego to the deeper or unconscious part oi the self. It shows how well the writer can integrate external forces within himself and therefore is the basis of our true inner security in the universe. Any weaknesses in the downstroke can show difficulties the writer has experienced with either or both parents.

It would show up as the bending or wavering of the stroke or in directional pressure. If pressure comes from the right, it would indicate insecurity arises from the father or the future. If from the left, insecurity arises from the mother or the past. The bent downstroke in the lower zone would reveal instinctual anxieties from either parent depending on the direction. Seen in the upper zone it would reveal fears connected to aspirations or values of the father.

The upstroke is the reverse in meaning of the downstroke. The upstroke into the upper zone is the means used to go away from the conscious self and the ego concerns toward the ideals and aspirations.

If one has difficulty rising into the upper zone it signifies struggles with the father and/or the family values. The upstroke coming out of the lower zone shows the capacity for actualizing or fulfilling the instinctual needs. This is the stroke that can show difficulties with either parent depending on how it is expressed. (ill. #6)

*Hoping the new year is good to you*

When considering slant and the parents we must remember that slant is one of the most consciously controllable graphic indicators. Its importance, therefore, is somewhat reduced. It does often show the nature of the adjustment to the father principle. Normal right slant expresses harmony with the father.

Left slant and to some extent upright slant can show resistance and struggle with the father, especially if this is confirmed in the lower zone. A contradiction in slant as seen in a conventional script with right slant in the middle and upper zone, but with a left slanted lower zone would show adjustment to the father on the social and intellectual level, but strong hostility on the unconscious level.

Extreme right slant in the lower zone shows unresolved problems with the mother. (ill. #7) Extreme right slant in the middle zone would show a father oriented difficulty with inner controls. Left slant in the middle zone shows emotional overcontrol, identification with the mother and resistance to the father.

Mixed slant can be a reflection of a struggle between the parents and the uncertainty in the writer as to which parent to identify with.

I have received your
letter the other day
stating that you were
going to appear on

## Movement And The Parents

The ability to move to the right rhythmically and purposefully shows the proper adjustment and basically good relationship to the father. Difficulties in moving rightward point to problems in relating to the father and possibly the mother. (ill. #8)

Being a child is a beautiful
thing ~ we all should allow

Most likely, it will reveal the inability to leave the security of the mother or show a continuing; attachment to early emotional needs that were not fulfilled. This is often seen in excess circularity, narrowness, and sluggishness of movement (not due to minimal brain damage) Excessive movement rightward shows a flight from the mother toward the father and implies a fearfulness or absence of a genuine emotional connection to the mother and to women in general.

This original insecurity will never let the write feel fulfilled in the father role because he is constantly running away from himself and his identity rather than building it up. The father identity cannot be true unless the initial mother connection is properly established. Any extremes in movement show difficulty with subduing impulses or channeling them properly. This can often be traced to poor or absent parental guidance or emotional insecurities based on the need for attention from the parents. (ill. #9)

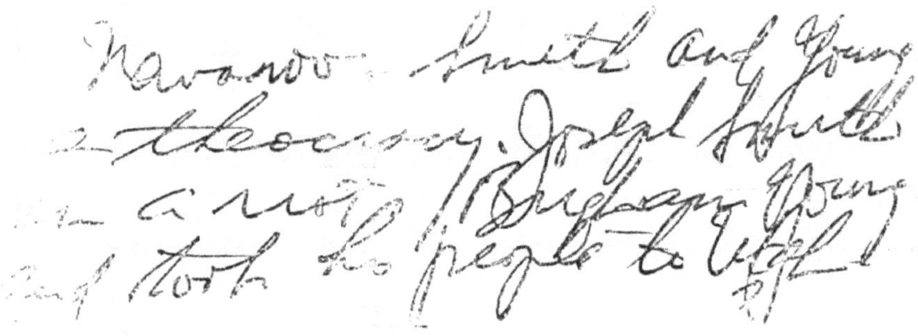

**Form and Parents**

Form, as Dr. William Hallow has pointed out, can be equated with the parent within, or the organizing principle that gives purpose to movement. Symbolically, movement would be the child within.

Form can also be considered as the ego or that which organizes the primal energy of the id. Since the ego formation is strongly influenced by the parents and the early environment, the writer's choice of forms can reveal the attitude toward the parents. Neglected forms can show early ego damage which has not been corrected. Middle zone forms showing low self-esteem may be the result of insufficient support, excessive criticism, or early rejection by the parents. (ill. #10)

Aside from the last week and the resultant strangeness, I feel much healthier and stronger than I was a couple of months ago when you were here - I ended my relationship with Mark

Poorly formed or disturbed shapes in the lov1er zone loops showing angular formations, twists, openings to the left, excessive pressure, etc., will indicate unresolved problems, often of an aggressive nature, with the mother that are influencing instinctual expression. Loops that are closed to low, are too small or narrow, or that cross to the right but then turn leftward away from the middle zone can show problems with father on the instinctual level. (see ill. #6) Rigid regularity of forms can reveal early demands for conforming to strict behavior patterns. (ill. #11)

Your pictures are faster than mine! Thanks so much for the print. It was really colorful. As you have noticed by now, I

If the script is strongly emotional and rigid as well it would show an upbringing that was not suited to the emotional needs of the child. School-type forms, especially in a good form level writing; would also show conservative home influences that were not helpful in developing the writer's individuality.

Artificial or persona writing can show an environment of social and emotional hypocrisy or a need for the child to act in a way different than he feels in order to win approval. Extreme disconnection would show lack of original emotional involvement with the mother. Roll-ins or hooks at the beginnings of words show anxiety regarding the mother and the fear of leaving the security of the early self. It also suggests unfulfilled needs in the mothering area. Claw strokes and other leftward movements at the end of words show an insecurity connected to the father. Excessive circularity shows unfulfilled oral needs or a basic disappointment concerning the amount of love received from the mother. This can be either aggressive or passive in nature.

Extreme height in the upper zone, especially with rigidity, can show strict authoritarian rules usually associated with the father; or it can reveal an emphasis on the non-emotional, especially if the middle zone is small and therefore shows problems in the emotional connection to the mother. Varying heights in the upper zone can show struggle with the father's rules and personality.

**Connections**

The preference for the arcade connection shows suppression of feeling and early difficulties in communicating emotions to and from the parents. The angular connection shows a preference for friction in emotional relationships and suggests that the writer experienced repression from a strong father figure. This will lead him to associate emotional response with strife.

A garland connection indicates that the writer's expression of feeling was given a more positive response and was permitted at least partial release. The garland is more feminine and emphasizes the relationship to the mother. The thread is the avoidance of friction and shows that the writer was compelled to find indirect expression or feelings or avoid them to a great extent. The thread also suggests difficulty in the proper ego formation.

### Space and Parents

The relationship to space is the last developed in the handwriting. It symbolizes the writer 's feelings about himself in terms of the greater world around him. It is indicative of his adjustment or lack of it to the social order. If there are signs of improper development in the earlier formative stages the writer will inevitably show problems in social or group adjustment. Lacking a proper mother and father connection, it is almost a foregone conclusion that the writer will have deep problems in social integration. (ill. #12)

to the city for a little ping-pong. This is first a note to

Disturbances in the rhythm of space is an important clue to the graphologist. It will lead him to search for the area in the writer's personality where progress was interrupted. Space rhythm is a secondary or confirming indicator when considering the parental influence in the script. Wide space between words or letters shows problems in initial emotional relationship to the mother.

Disorganization or lack of clarity in space distribution could reflect a state of emotional confusion in the early home environment coming from either or both parents. A wide or widening right margin could confirm a disturbance in the father relationship.

A wide or narrowing left margin could confirm insecurity patterns established through the mother. Avoidance of the lower portion of the writing area can confirm a fear of the instinctual and unconscious areas of the personality. This also would be mother-related. Tangled lines could confirm difficulties in expressing feelings in the early home. This also can be true of lines that are too far apart.

**The Capital "I" And The Parents**

It is believed by some graphologists that the parents can be seen in the capital "I." The father being the lower part of the form and the mother being the top part. This may have validity as a confirming indicator. It is not to be considered a primary expression of the parents in handwriting.

If one part of the PPI is overdone or neglected it symbolizes a corresponding influence from the parents. Distortion in the upper and/or lower part of the letter could indicate conflict between the parents, separation, or that their relationship was emotionally disturbing to the writer.

**Bibliography**

Dettweiler, Christian, *Jungen* In Not, pps.26-45

Adolf Bonz, Verlag, 1974

Hallow, William, Newsletter of the National Society for Graphology, May-June, 1974

Klein, Felix, Unpublished lectures presented in 1974

Mendel, Alfred, *Personality In Handwriting*, Stephen Daye Press, 1947

Witlich, Bernhard, *Neurosesstrukturen und Handschrift*

Dipa - Verlag, Frankfurt/Main. *Mysteries of Sexuality*

# Mysteries of Sexuality

# Sexuality–it all starts with the Male and Female Brains

*Hogamus Higamous, Men are Polygamous*
*Higamous Hogamous, Women are Monogamous*

Men and women are different and the chief reason is that the brain, the main administrative and emotional organ of life is differently constructed in men and women. It processes information in different ways, which results in different perceptions, priorities, and behaviors.

We share the same sexual identity for only the first few weeks after conception. Thereafter, in the womb, the actual structure and pattern of the brain begins to take a specifically male or female form. At about six weeks the male fetus develops the special cells which produce male hormone, the main one being testosterone which then stimulates the development of male genitalia.

The embryonic brain takes to time to acquire a sexual identity. If it is genetically female nothing drastic happens to the basic brain pattern. The natural template of the brain seems to be female. With boys it is different. Just as male gender needed the male hormone, so a radical intervention is needed to change the naturally female brain structure into a male pattern. Embryonic boy babies get a colossal dose of male hormone when the brains are taking shape. This second huge surge also occurs at the other end of male development, adolescence.

What creates a male or female brain is not genes, it is a matter of the degree to which our embryonic brains are exposed to the male hormone; a matter of the concentration, timing, and appropriateness of those hormones. Disturbances in the amounts of hormones can result in “female” identity in a male body or vice versa, and many other imbalances.

Scientists are beginning to believe that attention deficit problems and hyperactivity, dyslexia, stuttering, even severe mental disorders can be traced to faulty hormonal balances in the developmental stages. This is much more connected to be boys because they are the ones whose wiring has to be rearranged. Learning disorders, sexual deviations and severe psychosis are far more prevalent among males than females.

Some differences are apparent in the very first hours after birth. Girl babies are much more interested than boys in people and faces. The boys seem just as happy with objects dangled in front of them. One of the area's where the biggest differences have been found lie in spatial ability. That's picturing things, their shape, position, geography, and proportion accurately in the mind's eye.

This ability is related to mechanical and mathematical skill. At the top end of the scale of mechanical aptitude there will be twice as many men as women. Even in mathematical excellence the very best boys eclipse the very best girls. Also, the sex ratio for mathematical brilliance shows there are thirteen exceptional boys for every exceptional girl.

Boys also have superior hand to eye coordination which later relate to sports and physical activities. Seeing patterns and abstract relationships as in chess, even Russia where it is played nationally, males dominate.

While the male brain gives men the edge in dealing with things and theorems, the female brain is organized to respond more sensitively to all sensory stimuli. Women do better than men on tests of verbal ability and speak earlier as kids.

They are equipped to receive a wider range of sensory information and to connect and relate that information with greater facility, and to place a primacy on personal relationships and then to communicate. Females hear better than men. Six times as many girls as boys can sing in tune which relates to women being sensitive to the "tone of voice." They also smell more sensitively than men, see in dim light better than men and evidence seems to suggest greater acuity in taste, as well.

Women are better at noticing things, picking up social cues and nuances of meaning from tones of voice or intensity of expression. Because females use both sides of their brain more fluently they can perceive more globally. Women have a larger corpus callosum which allow for greater facility in the transfer of information between the two brain hemispheres and the ability to use both hemispheres simultaneously.

Women use the left and right sides more readily than men therefore there is less specialization. Women's language centers are on both sides of the brain, whereas with men it is on only one side. Brain specialization, or greater single mindedness and endurance related to higher levels of testosterone accounts for greater spatial and mathematical skill in males and less skill in language arts. Boys have a hormonal inlaid aggressiveness channeled into action, exploration, competition, and leadership. They want to assemble and disassemble objects. Girls prefer care taking games and domestic, less exploratory, and aggressive activities. Boys are inclined to settle arguments by fights or angry disputes, whereas girls are more likely to negotiate a conflict. Boys want to play with things, girls want to chat with people. For girls, popularity is more important than domination and leadership is associated with acceptability or social responsibility. Putting it simply men are preoccupied with things, theories and power and women more concerned with people, morality, and relationships. This underlies the many issues between the sexes.

Testosterone, the aggression and dominance hormone, is also the sex hormone in both sexes. Women can lose their ovaries which produce estrogen and still retain the capacity for sexual arousal But if they lose their adrenal gland, which produces testosterone their libido collapses. It can be restored by injections of testosterone.

A man's brain is better tuned to the effects of testosterone upon it due to its early influence in the womb. After puberty man has twenty times more of the substance in his body than does a woman. Aggression, dominance, and sex is a powerful mixture. The more the testosterone the greater the sexual urges.

Sexual awareness comes earlier in boys and is almost always more important to them. They are more sexually active than girls. They masturbate more frequently and, on average, have intercourse earlier. Love, or, at least, male lust, is blind. High testosterone acting upon the male brain increases the single minded approach to a problem, or the satisfaction of the sexual urge.

Men, being more hormonally driven are propelled toward the object, sometimes a variety of objects. Males are oriented toward promiscuity in their choice of sexual partners, as a result. Social restrictions act as a brake on this testosterone-fueled behavior.

In general, females are less interested in a variety of partners. This may also reflect the brain wiring urge of the male to increase the distribution of his DNA and increasing the viability of the tribal unit. The female wants to protect and nurture the fewer offspring she is capable of generating.

Mothers have forever warned their daughters that men are after only one thing, and they are usually right. Brain, body, and hormones combine to make the male sexually aggressive.

Men are much more willing to experience sex without love, impersonal and functional sex. A large majority of women reported that mere mechanical sex was highly unsatisfactory.

Men are more likely to see sex as a matter of objective things and actions. Starting in infancy they are as intrigued by a balloon as by a face. Not the case with girl infants who are much more drawn to faces and voices. Pornography is a turn on for most men. For most women the genitalia in pornography is not the attraction. Rather it is relationship of the people involved. Speak of Pfizer's attempt to create a female form of Viagra.

Sexual gratification matters less to women than it does to men. Men like sex because they are almost always guaranteed gratification. Only one fifth of women can claim an automatic climax. An overwhelming number of women cite affection and intimacy as their primary reason for liking sex.

Being gentled is the surer route to pleasure for women. The female orgasm rate is 17 times more likely in marriage while for men it is only nine times more likely. Put simply, men want sex, and women want relationships; men want flesh and women want love. Just as the boys wanted toys and carburetors, the girls have always wanted contact, communion, and company. The physical differences between the sexes attract men and women to each other. The psychological differences cause the mutual misunderstandings.

The female brain is not organized to keep sex in a separate compartment. That is more the male model. As if his brain has a specific filing cabinet for sex, unrelated to emotion.

Women are much less hit and run lovers. For them having sex with another is a manifestation of intimacy which cannot be abruptly shed. Women tend to be more practical with respect to matters of the heart than do men. The female brain is not blindsided by testosterone fueled desire, and is better equipped to analyze and rationalize emotions. In her brain the centers of reason and emotion are better connected.

It is to be hoped for that men and women can be more honest about what they actually feel and find ways to share and communicate their needs. And find a way to acknowledge the truth of their differences and work at finding more understanding and common ground. And, as well, strike a balance between love and ambition, and tenderness and striving.

**F-68 -** poor sexual identity

Good Morning Roger,

I am at school right now and two of my boys are playing the computer. St. Louis has had of a week off temperatures of 100° and better. Just to let you know, writing is not one of the things I like to do. Tomorrow we will be having a clown performance for the school and the little one are so looking forward to it. The grand kids of my adopted St. F St. Louis family will be performing with us and we will put a 45 min. show on for the pre-shoolers.

**M-25 -** more feminine than masculine traits

25-M

Thank you so very much for your services and willingness to assist in the endeavor. Your expertise was extremely valuable and appreciated.

I apologize for the delay in mailing; however the first letter was returned because I had forgotten to specify east or west in Regards to your street address.

However, once again thank you very much and I hope you enjoyed your stay in California.

Best Regards,

Joseph

Enclosure: (1) check

**M -** Masculine energy, but too much variability, showing ambivalence

you know how important
this is when I will write to
you in my own hand.
Thank you so very much
That's all
for the birthfest. It's
been a rough while ~~you~~ for
me and I really appreciate
your getting together with me
for friends food and fine beer.
I don't care what Connie or Kathy
say. As far as I'm concerned
you are one of the finest humans
beings I know. If Co. becomes too
much of a wan for you, give
me a call. Thanks again
Love John

**M-59-LH.** Aggressiveness

asked me to write a few
sentences so I will. Today I am
very busy. I have to make 10
phone calls as well as 3 meetings.
By the end of the day I will be
very tired, but I will cook dinner
for ma & I. She must ate & she
is working 11 hours today. I love
to see her in the morning & the night
She makes my life so much better.
So puts me in a peaceful state most
of the time

**M-45 .** Litigator

Hey Roger... In writing, please:
Moderate help is NOW NEEDED.

Age: 29 B-date: 5 July 69
Right handed. Absolutely stunning
looking!! No college, loves dogs, great
dresser, works out, married for 8
months, a sales-'saleswoman'(!!). Tom

**F-23** - Outer self-confidence, but cradle lower zone suggests strong need for nurturing.

Tom,

Just a little note to let you know what a great lunch I had with you. I really enjoyed it and we will have to go again.

Thanks again

[illegible]

**M -** Spends a great deal of time in his head.

4/21 → Defensive spiritual disciplines
→ Condition / cause / cures

condition
• Spiritual dryness, untreated, leads to intellectual doubt – no fault

• Belief in God vs. personal relationship of God: "spiritual deadness"

causes
• Don't always lead to S.D.
① Destruction of community (Individualistic)
– need to complement individual study w/ others
② Dissolution of the events of life (moralistic)
③ Physical deprivation (Dualistic)
– All is moral (buck up)
– All is psychological (listen, support)
– All is physical (Take meds)
NEED ALL

cures
Pour out soul
Remembers God's grace
Analyzes hopes
Preaches to own heart

① Pour out soul – keep doing it
– doing stuff → meditation, contemplation, prayer
② Remembers God's grace
③ Analyzes hopes (in God)
④ Preaches to own heart
"shut up", heart

→ Personal spiritual dryness reveals ... intellect-

Strong anxiety and strong drives

Dear Roger,

I have enclosed samples of my parents handwriting. They probably should have written a little more — I hope this will suffice.

I am anxiously awaiting our meeting on Tuesday August 15. I am very hopeful that you'll be able to help me in my search.

As far as old samples of my handwriting I couldnt locate any — if I do — I'll bring them on Tuesday.

Until then,

Louise [illegible]

High anxiety and shyness.

ear Roger,

I will be at your place on April 10th at 4pm. Inclu

here are 1) My information

2) A handwriting sample from my wife Hannah

3) A handwriting sample from my partners Bob Brown/St

4) The letter I wrote prior to our aborted meeting last tim

I have recently started a new company - our business is to buy, own, and lease out commercial aircraft. I have two partners who I have very good relations with. The samples of their handwriting is attached.

g sample from my wife Hanna

sample from my partners Bob Bro

wrote prior to our aborted meeting

new company - our business is

t commercial aircraft. I have

good relations with. The sampl

# Looking at Couples and Their Handwritings

# Looking At Couples and Their Handwritings

The emotional turbulence of love, coupling and marriage can be traced first to the issues of early sexual identity then to the way habits of the heart are shaped in childhood, and, finally to the inevitable changes that occur over the course of even the most successful relationships. The major themes-that all relationships must deal with are intimacy, sexuality, dependency, and work.

The psychoanalytic view of couples holds that each partner unconsciously gravitates to someone whom they see as fulfilling a deeply held need. The most powerful of. these needs exist in a state of tension: the desire for intimacy, on the one hand, and the need to establish one's identity as a separate person on the other.

This conflict is very much the same thing that all of us have had to deal with as children when our burgeoning self-hood was being formed. The recent work of psychologists Nancy Chodorow, Carol Gilligan, and Lillian Rubin sheds new light on the old questions about early gender identity. These writers believe that crucial experiences in the development of a child come much earlier and from a different source than did Freud, who felt that the resolution of the Oedipal conflict was the most important source of gender identity. Current thinking places much greater weight on pre—oedipal experiences.

It began by the asking of a simple question: "What is the effect on human development of the fact that only women do the mothering?" Whether in a boy or girl, the earliest, most primitive experiences of both attachment and identification are with a woman. It is a woman who is our first loved other, with whom we form a symbiotic bond within which we do not yet know self from other than self.

As we emerge from this undifferentiated state the mother remains as the primal experience of an internalized self. As we grow we must make a separation from the mother while yet maintaining some level of unity because we still remain critically dependent on the mother for a considerable period of time after individuation begins.

Carol Gilligan states the issue very well. "Relationships, and particularly issues of dependency, are experienced differently by women and men. For boys and men, separation and individuation are critically tied to gender identity since separation from the mother is essential for the development of masculinity.

For girls and women, feminine identity does not depend on the achievement of separation from the mother or on the progress of individuation. Since masculinity is defined through separation while femininity is defined through attachment, male identity is threatened by intimacy while female gender identity is threatened by separation. Thus, males tend to have difficulties with relationships while females tend to have problems with individuation" (See illustrations #1 & 2).

**Illustration #1**

The man (above) 39-L has had difficulty connecting to his feelings and forming lasting emotional bonds. His preference is for speed, angularity, narrowness, and simplification.

I live in what's known as a mobile home.
This semi-portable form of American housing evolved from
the old-fashioned trailer, the Windstream being the
archetypal example. Enter a Windstream and
you find yourself in a miniature and compact
world of dark walnut cabinets, lovely wood or
metal fixtures art-deco style.
But the new American mobile home is far

The woman (below) 38-L is unclear about her separateness and individuation. The confused space picture reflects problems in self-understanding.

So here is my sample handwriting
for you, my dear. It's enclosed with
the handwriting sample of my dear
friend, my new love, Billy Rather ~
so we can be analyzed together —
but you know what? I've just
noticed that my handwriting changes —
perhaps because I am left-handed?
Which means I can write upside down,
backwards, sideways - and always

**Illustration #2**

This is a well-adjusted couple. His roundedness, in addition to the right trend speed and simplification gives a good balance between warmth and achievement. Her garlands and regularity indicate nurturance and commitment. She makes it easy for his feminine side to express itself.

To my darling wife
goes my love and
all my wishes for her
happiness.

[illegible]

♂48R

If only to see clearer
the road my life is taking
Then it will make worth-
while all of its painstaking
For then I know just
what's in store, for all its
good and bad,
With hopes I'll know in
my life more happiness than
sad.

Cheryl C.

♀36R

Lillian Rubin, in her fine study, *Intimate Strangers*, notes that when a boy who has been raised by a woman confronts the need to establish his gender identity, it means a profound upheaval in his internal world. To identify with his maleness, he must renounce his connection with the first person outside himself to be internalized into his inner psychic world.

He must now seek a deeper attachment and identification with the father. But his father, until this time, has been a secondary character in his internal life, and a weak nurturing and emotional force. The boy needs his mother but can no longer be sure of her. In order to protect against this sense of deprivation he builds a set of defenses or ego boundaries that are relatively firm and fixed, that rigidly separate self from other, that not only limit his connections to others but also his connection to his own inner emotional life.

Men have a hard time relating emotionally and being in touch with their feelings. Women complain about this all the time. Because men are not good or comfortable in areas of emotional expression they turn their attention to matters they can do well–managing area such as work, finances, sports, areas that seem more subject to rational control. For a girl, the obvious similarities between herself and her mother make it easier to establish a gender identity. She need not displace the internalized image of the beloved mother and therefore has no need for the kind of rigid boundaries a man develops as a means of protecting his ego.

A woman's ego boundaries are more permeable and flexible than a man's. This means she will manage her internal and external life in ways so different than a man. A girl never has to separate herself as completely and as irrevocable as a boy must. She experiences herself as being more continuous with another. As a result, she will preserve the capacity born in the early symbiotic union; for participating in another's inner life, for empathic identification with another. The girl will later internalize the father as a loved other as well. When a boy internalizes father and banishes mother he is left with only one significant other in his inner life. For a girl there are two. This means that a woman's inner relationships are triangular while a man's remain dyadic.

Because of their connectedness to others the major problems for women center around maintaining separateness. Because of the need for differentiation is so strong in the early development the major difficulty for men is sustaining unity and relatedness. Separation from the mother occurs in both sexes at around the toddler period, but it can occur earlier if the infant and mother make a poor bond, with devastating effect on the psyche, especially in boys. This will result in a schizoidal neurotic character structure, where the individual is split off from his own feelings. The burden of separation is hard enough for boys even with a close mother connection, but experiencing it prematurely may be the reason that so many more men than women are both schizoidal and schizophrenic.

Dr. Rubin further says that women have the ability to find their way around human relationships and it enables them to deal with the demands of a variety of relationships with more comfort and ease than is possible for men. Men are not good at interpersonal relations that are loaded with emotional content.

The basic feminine sense of self is connected to others in the world, the basic masculine sense of self is separate. It follows from this that men have a harder time with intimacy than do women.

Think of it in terms of this definition of intimacy—the wish to know another's inner life along with the ability to share one's own. Now, men have an inner emotional life but when a relationship requires a sustained verbalization of that inner life and the full range of feelings that go with it they will find it quite difficult and burdensome. He can act out anger and frustration inside the family, but ask the man to express his sadness, his fear, his dependency, his vulnerability, and he's then likely to close down as if under some compulsion to protect himself.

There's an odd paradox here. All requests for intimacy are troublesome for a man, yet to the degree that it is possible for him to be emotionally open with anyone, it is with a woman ... a tribute to the power of the early childhood experience with the mother. Yet it is that same experience and his need to repress it that generates his resistance and ambivalence (See illustration #3 next page).

For a woman there is also a paradoxical side in her need for intimacy and emotional connection. Because her boundaries can be so easily breached she begins to fear that she may lose some part of herself. Unless she is vigilant she is all too likely to give herself away. For her, maintaining herself as a separate person in an intimate relationship is the dominant issue, the one she will struggle with from girlhood on.

Separation comes much later for her than for her brother. When it comes it is trough turning to the father that it is achieved. She will later turn to her husband as she did to her father to affirm her femaleness, her separateness, an integrity of self apart from the mother. It is this that propels women into marriage with such a sense of urgency and need for identity.

**Illustration #3**

The man's writing shows irregularity, disconnectedness with a poorly developed middle and lower zone. His behavior is unpredictable, and he avoids true emotional commitments due to identity problems. The woman provides mothering and long term care for this troubled man.

ILL#3

♂55R

Dear President Stein:

Your active support of the Brooklyn Loft Tenants is critical! I do urge and request that you give leadership to the fight to protect all of the tenants under the 1982 State Loft Law and to make the "grandfathering" zoning procedure available in Brooklyn as it was to thousands of tenants in Manhattan.

My best wishes to you for the New Year and success in your position as City Council President.

Sincerely,

♀36R

January 26, 1986

Dear Roger,

As I looked for examples of writings to give you, I realized over the years, the only writings I had were pages from diaries. And even my diaries had a poor showing in terms of quantity. As I was looking for samples to mail you, I felt practically everything was too personal. But I pulled out something from 1973 & 1974. By 1975,

The major components of love are intimacy, passion, and commitment. According to Dr. Robert Sternberg, a psychologist at Yale University, a relationship can survive with any two of these qualities, but the fullest love requires all three. Each of these aspects follows its own course and blossoms at its own pace. What brings people together initially, is not what keeps them together in the long run. Sternberg says that passion is the quickest to develop and the quickest to fade, intimacy develops more slowly, and commitment more gradually still. It is important that each partner have the capacity for change and growth. Of course, there is no assurance that either will grow in the same direction or at the same rate of speed.

No relationship is stable or unchanging because the basic components change at different rates and different intensities for each person. Relationships have to be worked at constantly. It cannot be taken for granted or it will become a hollow commitment, devoid of passion and commitment. It needs the kind of energy one puts into a career (See illustration #4 next page).

As an illustration of how the passion side of a relationship can fade and become less important, a study-done in 1978 found little or no relationship between frequency of sexual intercourse and marital satisfaction. In this study of 100 happily married couples 8% had intercourse less than once a month, and nearly a quarter had it only two or three times a month. Most couples reported having sex one to three times a week. Two of the couples had no intercourse and one couple had it every day. One-third of the men and two-thirds of the women reported having a sex problem. Yet those dissatisfied with their sex lives still felt their marriages to be working and happy.

**Illustration #4**

The man has angular and thready forms which show tension, insecurity, and ambivalence. He is not in touch with his or another's feelings. He is also very anal and controlling. The woman is exceptionally intelligent, caring, and responsible. She has a very high form level with the pictures of space, form, and movement all being strong.

ILL. #5

♂62R

The staunch clarity of some type
faces and the designs of some book and
posters have moved me too. The contents
of many books, science fiction, anthro,
poetry and Poetry (some) and ethos and
mythos and junk is source for lots
of ideas I've used ~~the accepted or rejected or used~~
~~t abused~~. Travel and towns and deserts,,
NYC Paris Amsterdam Rio Cusco L.A
Boston Mojave Washington Oregon

♀65R

October 24, 1985
131 Hope St,
Bristol, R.I. 02809
401-253-8267

Dear Roger Rubin,
I am writing to you for information
about a couple of problems that are
current in my life.
I have been working with two
women in N.Y., Alice Trillin and Jane
Garmey on a T.V. Series on Art for children.
I have produced 3 books on art for kids which
are tops in the field ...

This is a good place to say just-a few-words about sexuality in men and women. As was said before men repress their first identification with the mother and experience a muting of the emotional expression. This fits in nicely with cultural definitions of manliness that reduces the emotional in favor of the rational. Sex for men often becomes the one arena where it is legitimate for them to contact their deeper feeling states and to express them. For many men, the sex act carries most of the burden of emotional expression.

This may partly explain the urgency with which men so often approach sex. For women there is no satisfactory sex without an emotional connection, and, for a woman the connection must precede the sexual encounter. She wants to feel a sense of relationship even though it is transient. This harks back to the greater ease she had in incorporating both parents into her psychic reality and her greater freedom emerging and maintaining without defined boundaries (See illustration #5 next page).

The difference can also be seen in the way gay men and gay women relate. For men the fear of emotional attachment is paramount and therefore men have the ability to take pleasure in anonymous sex with little or no element of personal relatedness. This is so characteristic of male sexuality. Looking for an emotional connection through the act of sex and then immediately withdrawing behind their ego boundaries only to seek again and again in a compulsive search for fulfillment. With lesbians it is quite different.

**Illustration #5**

Both writers are artists. The man shows early developmental problems and emotional isolation. He was emotionally abandoned by his mother by the age of six months. Middle zone neglect, separation of letters, and very wide word spacing show this strongly. Intelligence is seen in clever and skillful simplifications. Over connectedness in the woman's script shows that she reasons out her feelings. She has a poor release pattern for her feelings.

♂62R

The storied clarity of some type faces and the design of some book and posters have moved me too. The contents of many books, science fiction, anthro, poetry and Poetry (some) and ethos and mythos and junk is source for lots of ideas I've used ~~I've accepted or rejected & used~~ & abused. Travel and towns and deserts,, NYC Paris Amsterdam Rio Cusco L.A Boston Mojave Washington Oregon

♀65R

October 24, 1985
131 Hope St,
Bristol, R.I. 02809
401-253-8267

Dear Roger Rubin,

I am writing to you for information about a couple of problems that are current in my life.

I have been working with two women in N.Y., Alice Trillin and Jane Garmey on a T.V. Series on Art for children. I have produced 3 books [illegible]

Sex generally is in the context of a relationship. Temporary, perhaps, but still some kind of a relationship. Lesbians can have intimate and satisfying relationships with each other without any sexual involvement. They tend to bond more readily and form long term partnerships or marriages of lasting duration much more often than gay men do.

Among gay men, a friendship that doesn't include sex is rare. The split between the sexual and the emotional is a dominant characteristic of male sexuality. Relations with other men relieve the pressure for an emotional connection that is always present in any interaction with a woman. This may, in part, explain why men seek more variety and novelty and have a harder time with monogamy than do women (See illustration #6 next page).

Dr. Otto Kernberg, a well-known psychoanalyst, had these interesting thoughts about sex. "Sexual passion reactivates the entire sequence of emotional states that assure the individual of his own, his parents, the entire world of objects' goodness and the hope of fulfillment of love in the face of frustration, hostility, and normal ambivalence". Passion in sexual love, in his view, is the result of a unique facet of mature loving relationships: the crossing of psychological boundaries between one's self and one's lover. The sense of becoming one with the loved person while simultaneously retaining a sense of oneself, generates a feeling of transcendence.

**Illustration #6**

Both writers have sexual identity difficulties. The man's script shows rigidity, fear of feelings, over involvement with the mother and sexual confusion. Look at the lower zone, upright slant, and left trend. The woman's writing shows neglect of form, unevenness of simplification and poor middle and lower zones; all lead to uncertainty of her sexual role.

Dear Roger,

♂46R Here is my first paragraph. I usually print so that is what I am doing now This gives you a sample of my writing

For this paragraph I will now write in script - which I never do unless I am in such a hurry I have no

7-7-83

♀42L Dear Roger,

I'm writing this letter in response to your request for a specimen of my hand-writing.

I'm also including my husband's handwriting as

I want to say a few words on the subject of dependence and friendship in relationships. All the research available show that married men live longer, healthier lives than those who are single. Among women, those who never marry have fewer physical or emotional problems than their married sisters. Widowhood can be difficult for both husbands and wives but the lifespan of the woman is not affected by the death of her husband, even if she doesn't remarry. The same is not true for men whose lives appear to be in some jeopardy if they do not marry again. Marriage benefits men in ways that women do not share.

Women are generally the ones to do chores of organizing daily life, of nurturing, of caring for a myriad of details in their joint social life. For a long time, the economic independence of men has been mistaken for their emotional independence, while women's economic dependency has been taken to suggest emotional dependence as well.

Women know, that despite the appearance they show to the world, their men are often like children in need. Women are usually the emotional ballast for their men, providing not just the stability they need but the place and the encouragement for the emotional expression that is unavailable elsewhere in most men's lives (See illustration #7 next page).

**Illustration #7**

The man's writing shows lack of emotional maturity, deep insecurity, and unresolved identity conflicts. This is seen in the mixed slant and problems in both the middle and lower zones. The woman's script is fluid,, aesthetic, and has zonal balance. She is supportive, loyal, nurturing and takes the controlling role.

♂33R

♂33R ILL #7 11/10/83

Dear Roger,

I am writing you from my office. I have been working here almost three weeks now. It has not been going very easily for me. I have doubts about whether or not I'm going to make it. I've bounced around so much in my life; and even though I always managed to do well initially, I haven't done anything at all yet. I have been in Real Estate for about seven months now and have not made one deal yet. I am losing confidence

Dear Roger –

♀32R I don't know if you remember our reading in March of 1981, but your "advice" and "forecasting" were instrumental in getting me together with the man you see before you!

Thank you for enlightening me.

If I could have one wish today, it would be that Sammy use his time with you to commit himself [illegible] ahead of him in life, and

It is an interesting conclusion drawn from studies of friendship from people of all ages and in all walks of life that women have more friendships than men and the difference in the content and quality of their friendships is also very marked. In Dr. Lillian Rubin's sampling over two-thirds of the single men couldn't name a best friend. Of those who could it was much more likely-to be a woman than a man who held that place in their lives. In contrast, over three-quarters of the single women had no trouble identifying a best friend and almost always that person was a woman.

Among those that were married far more men than women named a spouse as a best friend, their most trusted confidante, or the one they would be most likely to turn in emotional distress. For the married woman it was very different. Even when a woman did name her husband to one or more of these roles, it was never exclusively his. Most women identified at least one, usually more, trusted friends, and spoke openly and ardently about the importance of these relationships in their lives. Generally, women's friendships with each other rest on shared intimacies, self-revelation, nurturance, and emotional support.

In contrast, men's relationships are marked by shared activities dealing with work, sports, and sharing expertise. Their interactions were for the most part emotionally contained and controlled. When asked to explain why they didn't deal with more personal matters with their friends, some men were willing to admit that they couldn't share the pain they felt or risk allowing another man to see their vulnerability.

Men have a hard time telling other men about their fear of failure, disappointments in themselves, about always having to put on a show of strength and independence.

Men often have difficulties in developing friendships with other men because of the competitiveness that is built into male relationships. Women are so often the singular source of emotional support in the lives of their men. Many women know that the emotional vitality in the relationship comes from them.

In a recent report, Dr. Sternberg has found that the single most important element for the success of a romantic relationship was the sharing of ideas and interests with one's partner. Also important was the sense of growing personally through the relationship and taking pleasure in doing things for the other person.

According to Dr. Sternberg, "There is a basic core of what love is that is the same in any loving relationship whether with a lover or with one's child." That includes such elements as being able to count on the loved one in times of need; having a mutual understanding and sharing oneself and one's things with the loved one; giving and getting emotional support; promoting the welfare of the person; and, valuing and being happy with the person.

He further says that in a romantic relationship the single most important variable is how satisfied partners are with the match is whether they love each other in roughly equal degrees. The least happy situation is when one loves one partner much more or much less that the partner is perceived to love one in return. He has also found that women, but not men, feel it is their own unselfishness that is crucial to the success of a relationship. Women, traditionally, have been more the maintainers of relationships than have men.

# What Do Men Want?

## An Introduction to

## Male Gender Identity Issues

## for Graphologists

# Who Am I?

The answer to the question, "who am I?" can be answered in an astonishing variety of ways. The "I" is a composite of memories, experiences, selective fantasies, conscious and unconscious fears, achievements, associations, and cultural, social, familial, and parental influences. To others it is most often what you do and to yourself, it is too often what you intend to do. Through various models and mechanisms, we establish a sense of self which then gets carried with us into our perceptions and activities and ultimately, determines what we do and how well we succeed.

It is clear that identity includes considerably more than gender identity. But for men, the gender issue, or the idea of being a man, dominates the sense of personhood to a greater degree than it does in women. Men are more heavily invested in the stereotype of "manhood," its pride system and demands, than are women in the concert of "womanhood." Women's sense of identity, worth and purpose can be supported in many ways - attachments, achievement in work or other areas, and in multiple roles they will play. Because men are likely to interpret almost everything in terms of their manhood" men are more vulnerable than women and more easily threatened in their very core.

Current thinking on the development and formation of identity has been strongly influenced by feminist psychologists. Namely, Nancy Chodorow, Carol Gilligan, and Lillian Rubin. There seems to be a broad consensus on the way male identity is shaped Infants form a primary bond and attachment with the mother.

The infant clings to and totally depends on this nurturing and sustaining parent. At some point, usually at around three years old, the male child begins the process of separation that will lead to an independent self. Part of the process of individuation requires the child to become like the parent of the same gender. For the girl it is not necessary to undo her primary attachment and identification as a woman. She may separate her sense of a 'self' from that of her mother but even while doing so she continues her identification as a woman with the female parent. (ill. 1 next page)

The boy follows a more difficult route. Like the girl, he must detach himself in order to achieve independence, but he is forced to form another sense of gender identity. In learning to be a man, he must reject his earlier identity with his mother, which is then seen as "feminine," or as his being "Mamma's Boy" and not "masculine," and is therefore extremely threatening. During the period before puberty and, especially, after puberty the boy must establish his masculinity.

The problem he grapples with is that the earlier identification with the mother persists within him. It is never completely outgrown. In the search for manhood, any "feminine" traits or aspirations are viewed as womanly and threatening.

**ILL. 1.** Male. Age 60. Successful artist. Neglect of form and wide spaces between words show identity and separation problems with the mother that have never been properly resolved.

The staunch clarity of some type faces and the design of some book and posters have moved me too. The contents of many books, science fiction, anthro, poetry and Poetry (some) and ethos and mythos and junk is source for lots of ideas I've used ~~the accepted or rejected or used~~ & abused. Travel and towns and deserts, NYC Paris Amsterdam Rio Cusco L.A Boston Mojave Washington Oregon

**ILL. #2** Male. Age 43. English architect. Separated from mother but still yearns for her as seen in lower zone loops open to left. Has difficulty in sustaining long term relationships.

Alaska has slipped away to be mechanically filed
with my other trans-oceanic capers. Business trade has
necessitated my taking on more draughting staff but
this results in my increasing detachment from
the work while I continue to race about accomplishing
bugger all. Wendy's fireplaces stand unfinished – even

**ILL. #3** Male. Age 39. Sensitive, gentle, not homosexual. Has entered manhood without renouncing the creative and feminine.

umber & plywood

- not extremely active / thin market
- Pacific N.W. [Douglas Fir] 20 yr. growth time
- construction industry, building
- supply is fairly fixed
- major component is demand → housing sta
  fall off if interest rates are higher wh
  drop in lumber & plywood
- broad generalization · market follows interes
- difficult market to trade in · local floor

**ILL. #4** (Male. Age 43. brother to above writer. Has accepted and enforced rigid concept of masculinity by rejecting mother.

At long last I am setting down on paper the delicate strokes which bear my most profound and grim secrets. I do beg of you but one thing, and that is that should you surmise from herein that I be a dullard ~~and~~ for ego must an ordinary mortal

To prove himself a man, a boy must first prove himself "not a woman." He is in opposition to something that lives deep within him. He feels forever threatened in his gut, and essential identity by anything which reminds him of feminine behavior and his early feminine identification.

Chodorow says that "A boy, in order to feel himself adequately masculine, must distinguish and differentiate himself from others in a way girls need not - must characterize himself as someone apart. Moreover, he defines masculinity negatively, as that which is not feminine and/or connected to women, rather that positively." (ill. #3, #4)

In order to achieve a separate sense of self apart from his internalized mother he will be worked on by elements of his culture that are invested in his achieving manhood.

Manhood is something that must be attained and earned, something precious and fragile, something that must be defended. It is very distinct from the basic concept of femininity. Current anthropological research traces this phenomenon of masculinity in all many diverse cultures around the globe wherein a boy must "be made into a man." (ill. #5)

The methods of becoming a "real man" vary greatly from culture to culture. In our society we do not have clearly defined initiation rites such as enduring painful tattoos or killing a dangerous animal but we have a concept of what a "real man" is. He is strong, sexy, courageous, stoic, beneficent, modest, independent; sort of a leading man in Western movie.

**ILL. #5** Male. Age 51. Successful entrepreneur. Weak middle zone shows insecure identity. Driven to compensate by ambition and achievement, seen in the upper zone extensions.

**ILL. #6** Male. Age 62. Very energetic, driven, compulsive. Earns manhood by rigidly imposing self on others. Unyielding.

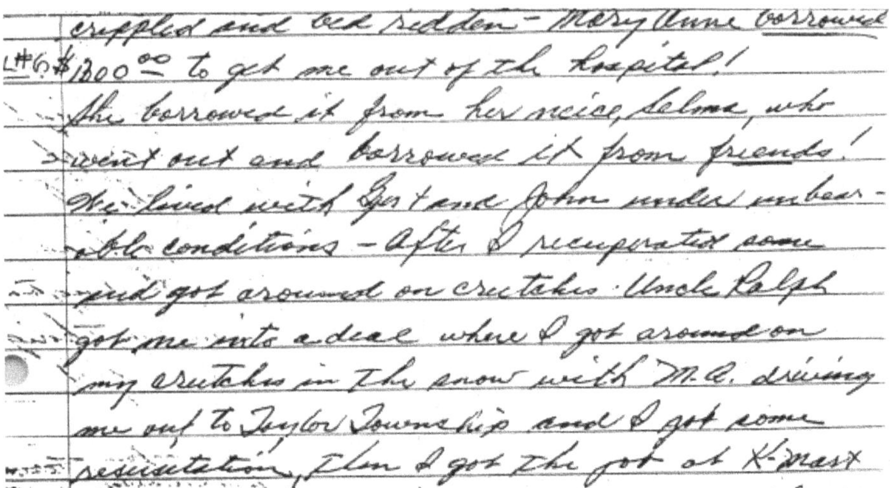

crippled and bed ridden - Mary Anne borrowed
L#6 $1300.00 to get me out of the hospital!
She borrowed it from her neice, Selma, who
went out and borrowed it from friends!
We lived with Gert and John under unbearable conditions - After I recuperated some
and got around on crutches. Uncle Ralph
got me into a deal where I got around on
my crutches in the snow with M.A. driving
me out to Taylor Township and I got some
resuscitation, Then I got the job at K-mart

He is not emotional, weak, and whiny, clinging, girlish, vain. He is not a Mama's boy. He must fulfill the conditions necessary for the three core roles of manhood: protector, provider, and procreator. Our society provides some symbolic indicators of the transition into manhood: first communion, confirmation, bar mitzvah, diplomas, and titles. But they are formal and contain very little substance and acknowledgment from the world of other men.

Getting a driver's license or the experience of sexual intercourse is more likely to provide the imprimatur of being a man, but it is personal rather than public. Each man must form his own self evaluations and seek reassurance from those around him. He is constantly alert to being judged and looking for signs of respect or disrespect in the search for validating his manhood.

Gaylin says it eloquently, "Lacking ceremonial liberations, each boy in our culture is required to find the door to manhood on his own. Whether freeing himself from hated parents or adored ones, he still has to escape from childhood and from the mother with whom he so lovingly first identified. With or without ritual, he must crawl toward that stereotype of masculinity by shedding the feminine parts of himself. Unfortunately, the feminine parts so shed may be fused with crucial capacities for love and tenderness, which in the process will also be abandoned." (ill. #7, #8)

**ILL. #7** Male. Age 38. Australian entrepreneur/marketing exec. Still has capacity for tenderness and nurturance intact. Always attracted to women who sought more macho types.

ILL#7 (7)

January 15, 1987

To Roger Rubin

Dear Roger:

Nice to chat again after so long. It's hard to believe that my last visit was August 84! There's a lot of catching up to do.

As I told you I spent my 43rd Birthday here in New York last December 86

I'm presently seeing a very lovely young doctor and our [illegible]

**ILL. #8** Male. Age 35. Partner to above writer. Weak male identity leads to exploitation and aggression. Winning is all.

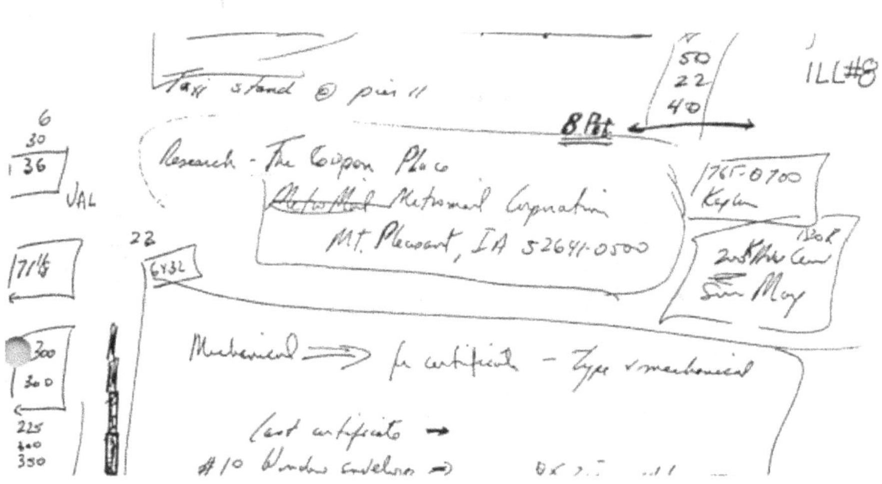


Genetic differences between boys and girls are apparent even at very early stages of development. Boys are born with a potential for larger body mass. Their verbal skills seem held back until a later stage of maturity. They are less analytical, and more kinetic/aggressive and competitive with their large motor skills dominant very early.

Genetic differences are seen not only in which games boys play but also in how they play them. Very early on girls veer toward conversation and communication. Their games tend to mimic life experience whether it be tea parties, playing house, dolls, doctor, or something else from the adult world of relationships.

It is true that little boys can enjoy cooking and crafts but they approach those activities very differently than girls do. They are so rules oriented that often rules are more important than the game. Boys will resolve conflicts in their games through appeal to the rules that govern it.

When the conflict can't be negotiated girls will simply disband the game. (ill. 9, 10)

While the way games are played may be genetically driven, what is being played is culturally influenced. Evidence suggests that aggression is often driven by androgen, the male hormone, so that brute power is the tool of the larger and stronger male.

Guile and negotiation must be substituted by the weaker muscled sex for there to be any kind of parity. In many ways this prepares women for modern life better than male biology does. Our world is not measured by the size of one's muscles, but by position, accomplishment, and intellectual achievement.

**ILL. #9** Male. Late 60's. Henry Kissinger. Tense, cautious, original. Operates in the realm of rules and ruthless competition. Defines how game is played and then plays it to win.

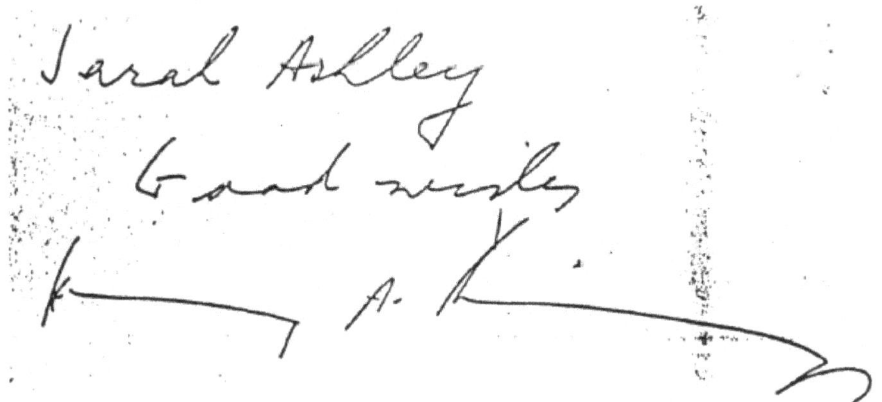

**ILL. #10** Male. Age 37. French banker. Very successful. Control, structure, abstractions are where he lives. The emotional, the compassionate, the feminine are rigidly suppressed.

Dear Michael

Just a quick note to enclose our annual report which I thought you might enjoy perusing as there are some great pictures of our new "building."

Also of interest is page 27 which mentions the two areas where I worked/work: ITM Ltd in the left column and Private Banking on the right.

We look forward to seeing you, Tracey and Philipp in early July.

Lots of love,

**ILL. #11** Male. Age 42. Successful lawyer. Sensitive, empathic, and a skilled negotiator. Combines masculine and feminine polarities effectively at work and at home.

Both my mother and father
were born in Europe and
I have spent a considerable
amount of time there — so maybe
this influences my thinking.
I am enclosing my resume
to give you a further picture of
my career to date. My problem
at this point is that I have been
in a large firm, a corporation
and of solo practice and I
see problems with each. I have

The early lessons little boys learn about becoming men can become the spears on which their self-respect will be impaled later on. In a cultural sense, if we as a society decide it is essential to live in a less aggressive society we can modify the soft wiring of genetic instruction and begin to reward conciliatory behavior in boys while discouraging crude aggressiveness. To some small extent this is now being done. (ill. 11)

A man's personhood is his manhood. His sense of pride is always tied to the larger environment of other men where power, status, and position in the world are the measure of being a "real man." In our upwardly mobile society there is a competitive, constantly challenging group of men to strive against and to be overtaken. The need for further victories is unceasing. On the other hand, if a woman is forced to establish her worth only in terms of her relationships with others, at least she can point to many others: women friends, children, lovers, family and of course men.

If there is a touchstone that marks a woman's femininity it is likely in her sense of her loveability, her capacity for giving and for maintaining relationships. (ill.12)

Women tend to feel shamed when there is a failure in a relationship or when the attachment bond is threatened. Her shame is the failure to live up to the inner ideals of nurturance and bonding. When women commit suicide it is usually related to the depression caused by the loss of a loved object. Men commit suicide at a higher rate of frequency than women do in our culture.

**ILL. #12** Male. Late 30's. Stockbroker. Aggressive, competitive, and very driven. In his jungle the ends justify the means. Can never relax because another man might beat him out.

You should explain
precisely the situation
as it was explained to you
(in written form if necessary)
stating that after thorough
checking it is our view that
floor broker was acting within
all rules, & effectively under circs.

They so often do it because of perceived social humiliation tied to business failures. Men become depressed because of loss of status and power in the world of men. It is not the actual loss of money or material benefits that causes the despair, it is the shame and humiliation and failure a man feels when he has ceased being a "man among men;" that he has a profound flaw at his very core which is beyond remedy.

The following excerpt from Michael Herzfeld's The Poetics of Manhood: Contest and Identity in a Cretan Mountain Village, will illustrate the rituals of manhood in a pre-industrial society. Remnants of the same criteria exist today in our complex urban culture. Although current customs seem less well defined they can be traced back to the same sources as evidenced in the action adventure hero types on the TV and movie screens.

"One who is 'good at being a man' must know how to wield a knife; dance the acrobatic steps of the leader of the line; respond in elegant, assonant verse to a singer's mockery; eat meat conspicuously whenever he gets the chance; keep his word but get some profit from it at the same time; and stand up to anyone who dares insult him.

He must protect his family from sexual and verbal threats; and keep his household at a level that befits a "master of the house." He must dispense hospitality while depreciating the poverty of his table as he plies his guests with food and wine.

He must be ready with clever humor. And in all these domains, his every action must proclaim itself a further proof of his manhood. An action that fails to point up its own excellence is like the proverbial tree falling in an empty forest.

**ILL. #13** Male. Age 45. Organic farmer. Dropped out of main stream due to pressure of the "rat race." To avoid acting out his aggression, he left the tensions and threats of urban life.

Greetings Roger — 6 Dec 90

Hope this finds you well and in tune. Enclosed is our latest Family Portrait. Pretty wild year - Bush wise hope we get out of this one. Wheres Andy - when we need him - he would have made such a great political figure. We have organized one peace vigil in hardwicke trying to organize people to let there fathers in D.C. about how we [illegible] Farm... [illegible] on and [illegible]

In most pre-industrial cultures one of the first measures of a man was his capacity to procreate. His adequacy, his "real manhood" was demonstrated by having many children, and for that he may have been entitled to more than one wife. This would give evidence of his potency, which is not merely fertility but the ability to "get it up," to penetrate the woman, to express his "manliness."

Men are inordinately concerned about penis size as a measure of power and so many suffer anxiety about comparing their size to another's. This has nothing to do with giving pleasure to a woman because for women size is rarely a top priority. Rather, it has to do with measuring, competing and inner validation in the world of other men.

The penis is the symbol of male power and authority, the phallus, the erect penis, is the performing instrument. Impotence in any area of activity is visualized as. A reflection on sexual potency, which is the foundation of manhood. Sexuality for too many men is stripped of its pleasure function in the service of gender identity. It is perceived as a conquest and a victory and often leads to philandering and casual sexuality. By turning sex into yet another index of status and power, men destroy the joyful and tender aspects of the most intimate of human experiences.

Another major role assigned to man is that of protector. Man must be a warrior. He must be powerful and must demonstrate his power whether in a hunting or non-hunting society. Ultimately, mastery must be demonstrated on the physical level. An essential ingredient of the protector is the demonstration of courage and it is always visualized on the level of the primitive and the physical.

In the modern world there are few direct threats to physical survival. Men are more likely to feel threatened when they sense disapproval, exploitation, frustration, betrayal, or humiliation. Fear and anger were intended as responses to threats to our very survival, not as appropriate reactions to pride, status, position, dignity, or manhood. Affronts to a man's status is responded to with biological defenses appropriate for physical assaults.

In today's world physical courage might prove life threatening rather than lifesaving. Most often what men feel today is less the need to show courage than the fear of showing cowardice. (ill. 13)

By contrast, women do not feel they must be brave or courageous, which does not mean they lack these virtues. Rather, they do not measure themselves exclusively by that standard. Consequently, they do not fear the exposure or failure as a shameful flaw at their very core. Aggression in all animals is influenced by male hormones. On the physical level, women are less aggressive than men. It doesn't mean less assertive, nor does it deny the existence of aggressive women.

Aggression, violence, and power do not enhance survival for women. The differences in body size and strength put women at risk in a contest with men. A genetic endowment for direct confrontation and attack is maladaptive. A smaller person would lose in direct combat. A better survival mode would be intelligence, rationality, accommodation, pleasing, willingness, and ingratiation. Women are better able to admit vulnerability, which also gives rise to compassion for the weakness of others. The role of provider is crucial to a man's self-respect, pride, and status. Work may be the single most important underpinning to a man's sense of his intrinsic worth.

Pride is built on work and achievement and the success that results from that work. This, in spite of the fact that many men today are ambivalent or confused in their attitudes toward work. Without work or the essential identification that comes from work most men will withdraw into feelings of self-contempt and humiliation. Even unrewarding work is better than no work at all. Hopefully, it will provide some pleasure of mastery.

For men, unlike women, work defines their manhood. Even if the work is without pleasure, or an alternative money source is available, such as a working wife, the idled man perceives himself as being incomplete. His ego, his essential self, demands that he be a breadwinner, that he show his ability to provide, that he be self-sustainingly independent, that he be a man and not a weak, needy boy.

The role of warrior has little direct translation into the conditions of modern day living. The role of provider, on the other hand, is fully understood. It is necessary to support basic survival and other needs or desires. These other needs usually feed into the areas of status, competition, and self-worth.

The loss of a job is almost always interpreted by men as a failure of the essential self, and it can unleash a torrent of shame. His fear of failing as a provider is equivalent to the terror more primitive man felt when he saw his food supply disappear. Although most work has been reduced to mere labor, a hunt without glory, its loss is much more than a financial problem, it is a blow to pride and self-respect. When a man loses his job or is forced to retire he feels the guilt of failing in one of his primary responsibilities, and he often interprets this as a sign of impotence. It erodes self-respect and confidence and leads to depression and suicide. As mentioned before, the leading cause of suicide in men is failure in the work place.

Life and relationships for both men and women are controlled by a gender identity undercurrent. These are unconscious, polarized defenses that are usually experienced as protective and life preserving. The reality is that these defenses keep us locked in patterns of automatic behaviors that are as hard to modify and are as destructive as addictions.

**ILL. #14** Male. Age 80. Critic, philosopher, creative writer. Is deeply invested in the world of the mind. Distrusts the emotional in his own life. The intellect is preferred, as the safer instrument, over the feelings.

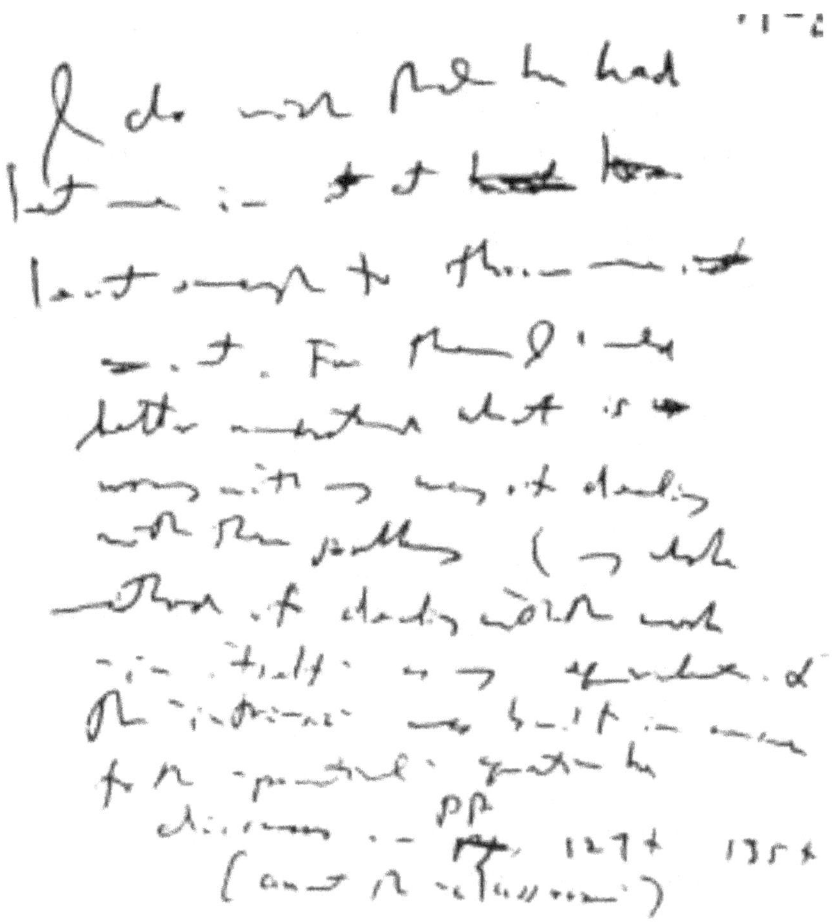

**Destructive addictions characteristic of males are:**

**DEFENSIVE AGGRESSION**: the need to deny fear or "unmanliness" produces a rigidly competitive, hyper aggressive state that makes a man self-hating when he loses, and compulsively self-protective toward a world he experiences as a dangerous jungle. It also makes him prone to self-destructive anger when frustrated and unable to turn away from challenges without feeling diminished.

**DEFENSIVE CONTROL** creates a never ending need to control, and avoid everything where control is not possible. It creates a boundless ego and a compulsive need to impose oneself on everything. This, along with the inability to hear and take in other people's reality or share psychological space, sets up resistance to submission and an intolerance of ambiguity and vulnerability.

**DEFENSIVE AUTONOMY**: produces a desire for self-containment, distance, and space; an intolerance of weakness and inner needs; a compulsion to become stoic; an inability to ask for help; an avoidance of personal connection or bonding unless it is based on "using;" an absence of playfulness.

**DEFENSIVE RATIONALITY**; leads to separating from the personal and emotional because it cannot be controlled by the intellect; a preference for objects over people; using logic as a weapon and distrusting anything not objective. (ill. 14)

**DEFENSIVE SEXUALITY** compulsive behaviors and obsessive preoccupation with sex; sex is used primarily as tension release and as a way of avoiding connections to another; thinking that only good sex can produce a good relationship with a woman.

**DEFENSIVE MACHISMO**. the compulsive and insatiable need for self-validation of manliness, which is designed to deny the powerful unconscious female imprint within.

The following is quoted from the last paragraphs of Willard Gaylin's *The Male Ego*:

"The liberation from the daily struggle for survival should have left us freer to pursue pleasures and activities that enhance the ego and enrich the soul. But we have created a society which seems to corrupt true pleasure, and we contaminate all of our activities with the insistence that somehow or other even play, even love, must be subsidiary to supporting our manhood. Everything is subjugated and abased in the service of supporting the fragility of the male ego.

"In the last generation we have seen women struggle to overcome the oppression of gender stereotyping; to liberate themselves from men's views of their proper place. Many women have deluded themselves into feeling that only they had been given the dirty end of the stick. They assume their sufferings will end when they seize the initiatives, the roles, and the identities that have been exclusively a masculine preserve.

"They are rushing into the world of men. Be cautioned. It is a world with its own variety of humiliation and its own brand of grief. We have created a society in which there are no victors, only victims. The role of man in our culture may be the role of privilege, but it is not the role of pride.

"Because men have been vested with the power over the fate of our culture, indeed our planet, the thrashing of a male ego in decline may destroy us all. We must begin to redefine manhood in terms that are achievable; with conditions that will nurture and sustain us all, men and women. Our civilization may depend on it."

The following is a selected list of male attributes, taken from Muller-Enskat's "Male and Female" symbols printed in Felix Klein's, Male and Female in the Handwriting.

**General Attributes**

Strength and force with little flexibility, concentration, and directness, tends to be opinionated, life lived from inside toward outside (centrifugal), active, pressing, restless, roving. Danger of a life of adventure, unbalanced, complicated, original, prone to conflicts, contradictory. Seeks knowledge, action, achievement. The legitimate, the predictable, the formed, and the conventional will be valued higher than manifold impressions and organic growth. Relationship to the past and future is stronger than the relationship to the moment, "to be above the situation."

There is a danger of lack of realism toward life and danger of partiality. Sexual drive or force, desire for ecstasy, eager for conquest and combat.

**Graphic Characteristics:** Dynamic, wide ranging, sure, upright, definite, self-reliant, clear, regulated, precise, concise, sober, cool, hard, angular, spasmodic, impetuous, wiry, deliberate, not genuine. Emphasis on form, high degree of rigidity, strong rhythm, originality, lacks uniformity.

**Mode of Perception:** Critical, differentiated, objective, logic, power of observing, concentration, purposeful thinking, intellectualism, dogmatism, preference for theories.

**Ego Structure:** Autocratic, certainty, pride, feeling for honor, ambition for achievement, inclination for power, leans toward making projections and repressions.

**Relationship to Environment:** Open to distant worlds, prefers the factual, imposes self through interference and domination. Technical and specialized interests, isolates self and stays at a distance.

**Emotional Disposition:** Tendency for passion, patriarchal sense for responsibility, love for profession and love of facts, little sensibility and little empathy, bluntness, coldness,

## BIBLIOGRAPHY

Chodorow, Nancy. *The Reproduction of Mothering: Psychoanalysis and the Sociology of Gender.* Berkeley. Univ. Of California Press, 1978

Gaylin, Willard Gilligan. Carol Goldberg, Herb. *The Male Ego.* New York. Viking Press, 1992

*In A Different Voice.* Cambridge. Harvard University Press, 1982

*The Inner Male.* New York. New American Library, 1987

Herzfeld, Michael. *The Poetics of Manhood: Contest and Identity In a Cretan Mountain Village* Princeton, NJ. Princeton University Press, 1985

Klein, Felix. *Male And Female In the Handwriting.* Monograph, 1972

Miedzian, Myriam. *Boys Will Be Boys.* New York. Doubleday, 1991

Osherson, Samuel. *Wrestling With Love.* New York. Ballantine Books, 1992

Rubin, Lillian. *Intimate Strangers.* New York, Harper & Row, 1983

# Narcissistic and Borderline Personality Disorders

Roger Rubin

# Narcissistic and Borderline Personality Disorders: a Graphological Perspective

When looking at the narcissistic and borderline disorders some commentators note the difficulty in making precise distinctions and diagnostic categories that distinguish them. There is often an overlapping mixture of behaviors, symptoms, and features with other disorders.

Alexander Lowen considers the borderline condition only one of five points on the narcissistic continuum. In increasing order of disturbance, he lists the Phallic-narcissist, narcissist, borderline, psychopathic, and paranoid personalities. Heinz Kohut, Otto Kernberg, and James Masterson all discuss the complexity of diagnosis and treatment. *The DSM III* refers to three clusters of personality disorders and one of those clusters includes Antisocial, Borderline, Histrionic and Narcissistic types.

The character disorder is generally thought of as having been formed earlier in the developmental sequence, i.e. prior to the oedipal stage, than neuroses which are formed during the oedipal period.

Narcissistic and borderline disorders are becoming more popular, or, perhaps, more fashionable as a label used by psychologists and psychoanalysts. These labels and problems were not the stuff of Freud's early observations and theories. A hundred years or so ago the typical neurosis was hysteria which resulted from a damming up of sexual energy often leading to conversion symptoms such as paralysis, blindness, or other physical symptoms without any physical basis. These led Freud into the exploration of neurosis and psychoanalysis.

At that time, culture was defined by strict class structure, respect for authority, prudery, and a repressive sexual morality. This produced in many a heightened superego with intense guilt and anxiety about sex and sexuality. Today, a century later, an enormous cultural shift has occurred and is marked by a breakdown of authority both in and out of the home.

Handwritings in the U.S. one hundred years ago were characterized by control, regularity, rigid adherence to school models and a marked suppression of individuality. In the decades after the second World War sexual prudery has been replaced by casualness, exhibitionism, and pornography. Fewer people suffer from conscious guilt or anxiety about sex. We hear a great deal about sexual dysfunction and inadequacy in performance.

Lowen writes, "Victorian culture fostered strong feelings but imposed heavy restraints on their expression. This led to hysteria. Our present day culture imposes fewer restraints on behavior and encourages the "acting out" of sexual impulses in the name of liberation but minimizes the importance of feeling. The result is narcissism. One might say that Victorian culture emphasized love without sex, whereas our present culture emphasizes sex without love." He further states that The descriptive term "character disorder" is often explained in a relatively simplistic way by contrasting it with the idea of a neurosis. A person with a character or personality disorder blames his problems and anxieties on persons or conditions outside of himself. The neurotic tends to blame himself for the emotional distress he is feeling, i.e. something is intrinsically wrong with him and his symptoms are caused by him.

Because of this sense of personal responsibility, the neurotic is more likely to attempt solving problems by working on himself. This suggests the presence of a more observant self and a more developed ego structure. In a therapeutic setting it allows for greater ease in transference or forming an alliance with the psychotherapist. The "character disorder" individual will be very much less inclined to enter therapy, acknowledge the need for change from within, and prove a much more intractable, difficult patient and therefore less likely to benefit from therapy.

When looking at the narcissistic and borderline disorders some commentators note the difficulty in making precise distinctions and diagnostic categories that distinguish them. There is often an overlapping mixture of behaviors, symptoms, and features with other disorders.

Alexander Lowen considers the borderline condition only one of five points on the narcissistic continuum. In increasing order of disturbance, he lists the Phallic-narcissist, narcissist, borderline, psychopathic, and paranoid personalities. Heinz Kohut, Otto Kernberg, and James Masterson all discuss the complexity of diagnosis and treatment. The *DSM* refers to three clusters of personality disorders and one of those clusters includes Antisocial, Borderline, Histrionic, and Narcissistic.

"Power, performance, and productivity have become dominant values replacing such old fashioned virtues as dignity, integrity, and self-respect." The focus is on private ambitions, loss of concern for the needs of others, and a demand for immediate gratification. This also resonates with Erich Fromm's concept of the "marketing type" as a product of 20th century western culture. The marketing man reshapes his identity by adjusting himself to the demands of the market place, the job, or other external demands. Graphologically this would show in a high degree of fluidity, reduced sense of form, and increased thread, speed, and other signs of superficiality.

The label narcissistic means more than mere egocentricity which can be found in all individuals who are driven primarily by their needs and anxieties. Narcissism, as a character disorder, refers to those individuals who overvalue their personal worth, who direct their affections toward themselves rather than others, and expect that those others will not only recognize but cater to the high esteem in which the narcissist holds himself.

The narcissist's character is based on a defensive false self that must be kept inflated, like a balloon, so as not to feel the underlying rage and depression which results from a sense of inadequacy and a fragmented sense of self. The narcissist's inflated false self is typified by an apparent imperviousness to depression. By contrast, the borderline is preoccupied with the fear of and vulnerability to an abandonment depression. The narcissist is motivated by a continuous need to reinforce his grandiosity and sense of self-importance.

They think of themselves as "extra-special" individuals who are entitled to unusual rights and privileges. They tend to be restless and driven, constantly pressured to maintain the sense of grandeur. They easily rationalize deficiencies and can manufacture grandiosity over the smallest of accomplishments. Many will be workaholics especially if they do a job well. Not being an achiever does not fit into their self-image.

It is important to remember that there is a healthy narcissism without which we could not derive the positive feelings necessary for self-esteem and self-assertion, and for the pursuit of special interests and ambitions. Constructive narcissism is being able to identify what you want and need, energize yourself and strive for it, while taking into account the welfare of others.

An example that Masterson uses to describe healthy and unhealthy narcissism is in lecturing to a group of people. It is healthy when the motive is to present ideas to stimulate and educate the audience and derive gratification from doing this. If the motive for lecturing is merely to exhibit the speaker's greatness then the audience's role is not to learn but to mirror the speaker's self-importance, then the narcissism is an expression of some degree of character disorder.

The legend of Narcissus reveals the core issue of the problem. Narcissus rejected the love of Echo very heartlessly and the Gods decided to punish him with an unreciprocated love by having him fall in love with his own beautiful image when he saw it in reflection, mirrored in a quiet pool. His reflection deceives him because it shows only his perfect and wonderful side and not his other parts.

His back view, and his shadow, in the Jungian sense, remain hidden from him. His self-rapture is the equivalent of grandiosity. He denied his true self, wanting to be at one only with the beautiful picture. His death is the logical consequence of the fixation on the false self. He was unable to deal with the unacceptable feelings of the self from which he tried to escape such as impotence, shame, envy, jealousy, confusion, and mourning.

The narcissist has an insatiable craving for adulation and mirroring, and needs praise to feel good about himself. Those who function at a high level are often in professions that supply these needs. Acting, modeling, politics, performance arts, sports and other exhibitionistic activities are ideal outlets. This work environment is very protective because it offers the continuous feedback that keeps the balloon inflated.

Interpersonal exploitiveness is very characteristic. Narcissists use others to indulge their desires and expect favors without reciprocal exchanges. This can lead to antisocial behaviors where ordinary rules do not apply. Since narcissists have little social conscience they are insensitive to what others need and feel. Their reaction to being hurt, disapproved of, or rejected is sharp rage or deep depression. Their depression is usually short lived as they are adept at finding ways to establish a positive mirroring of themselves either through self-deception or manipulation of others.

Wilhelm Reich introduced the idea of the Phallic-Narcissist character type. This refers to the behavior of those whose egos arc invested in the seduction of the opposite sex. Lowen believes this type to have the strongest ego structure and the least degree of disturbance.

Some confusion may arise in differentiating the histrionic or hysteric personality from the narcissistic. A distinguishing feature of narcissists is their desire to avoid dependence on others and view themselves as cool and above the responsibilities of shared living. By contrast, hysterics, though very much in need of recognition and applause can be warmly expressive, and often seek close, if only fleeting relationships. They are willing to work within the conventions and fashions of social life especially if it gives them the hope of getting the approval and attention they desire.

Hysterics can have some capacity to relate to another object.

If narcissists experience continued adversity and failure they can fall into a condition of paranoid disorder. When their image of superiority and omnipotence has been undermined they create a compensatory delusion of grandiosity. They believe they are special and others are conspiring against them. There is a marked split between ego image and real self.

This can lead to full-fledged paranoia and deep psychosis. It represents the highest degree of narcissistic withdrawal into the self. The narcissist's inflated false self is traceable to the early mothering experience. A perfectionist or narcissist mother needs a perfect child to act as a mirror for her own perfectionist self-image.

The child can be pampered and indulged in ways that teach him that he can receive without giving in return, and he deserves prominence without special effort. Some mothers are angry or rejecting if the child does not live up to her expectations. The child's fused symbiotic image he holds of himself and his mother is never separated. The mother's failure and imperfections are never acknowledged as that would bring on depression.

This represents a developmental arrest. The child identifies with the omnipotent mother image who can do anything, and required of him perfection and grandiosity for her own mirroring. In reality this is an angry and attacking mother who disapproved of any self-expression other than along the lines of her own image of perfection. This becomes the basis for the child's relationship to others: when they mirror his grandiosity he likes them, when they frustrate his need for mirroring he attacks or devalues them.

The term "borderline" was created to describe an intermediary degree of personality functioning that lies somewhere between neurosis and psychosis. The borderline, like the narcissistic disorder, is believed to have been formed in the pre-oedipal period. If the narcissist has an inflated false self then the borderline suffers from a deflated false self. The purpose of the false self is not adaptive as would be found in a healthy ego, rather it is for defense. It protects against painful feelings. Masterson says, "The false self does not set out to master reality but to avoid painful feelings, a goal it achieves at the cost of mastering reality."

One of the first issues a child learns to deal with is the problem of separation. Being left for certain periods of time is followed by the return of the mother and reassurance and reestablishment of the bond.

Playing the game of peekaboo is a way of helping a child deal with separation. The borderline faces this issue in a very extreme way.He experiences the mother as being unavailable to supply emotional nourishment and assurance and from this he feels he has been abandoned. This abandonment experience results in the child engaging either in intense clinging and dependency behaviors, or in equally strong distancing behaviors.

The child's psyche becomes fixated at this point in development. As a response to the mother's mixed signals the child's clinging brings fears of being taken over or engulfed. He then defends against this by distancing himself emotionally from the mother, and others, as well, because he fears abandonment. Getting locked into these powerful emotional swings means being stuck and giving up further growth and individuation. The borderline is constantly feeling an underlying abandonment depression.

Most of his characteristic behaviors stem from this condition. It is as if he experiences that an essential part of the self is lost or cut off from supplies necessary to sustain life. Masterson says "abandonment depression is actually an umbrella term beneath which ride the six horsemen of the Psychic Apocalypse: Depression, Panic, Rage, Guilt, Helplessness, and Emptiness."

The functions of the ego which include reality perception, frustration tolerance, and stable ego boundaries only cane about when separation from the mother succeeds. Then individuation can proceed. The borderline finds himself in a state of great emotional turbulence swinging back and forth between the good mother from whom he demands love and to whom he clings, and the bad mother from whom he must pull away.

This splitting is one of the borderline's principal defenses. It follows from this that they have considerable difficulty in maintaining a stable sense of who they are and a sense of personal identity. Although some borderlines function quite well, most will be found operating below their achievement potential whether it be scholastic, marital, or vocational.

Mood swings, poor impulse control, fluctuations in concentration, hyper sensitivity to rejection or criticism, the need to appease others and the subsequent rage at not getting desired responses keeps their performance levels uneven and restricts achievement. They don't handle routine well, have difficulty in developing insights, are inclined to lead chaotic lives, and have little empathy for others.

The borderline plays out the painful parental relationship with another person cast as the parent. For instance, a clinging borderline wife idealizes a narcissistic husband, using his sense of superiority to shore up her inadequate self.

She is compliant, subservient, eager to give him what he wants, but she always fails to meet his standards. The husband attacks her for her inadequacies and reinforces her negative feelings about herself. Borderlines act out in other ways that are often self-destructive or anti-social. Alcohol, drugs, excessive work habits, and other addictions serve as distractions from depression. They are driven by the pleasure principle, by a superficial kind of feeling good as a way of avoiding pain. It produces a temporary sense of "clinging," a feeling that something outside of himself will provide support, rescue, or happiness to take away the anxiety. Many borderlines wind up as cult followers, or connect to groups with strict rules as mother substitutes.

The schizoid has a close resemblance to the borderline. The schizoid type is characterized by emotional coldness and aloofness, indifference to either praise or criticism from others, and few, if any close friendships. The primary defense that the schizoid relies on is that of distancing and isolating the self from the internal emotional Object. The overriding anxiety centers around being controlled, and ultimately, engulfed with a total loss of self and identity. It is the fear of the invasive parent crushing and absorbing him. This leads to fear and avoidance of closeness and an extreme emotional remoteness. The rage and turbulence of the borderline are not in evidence.

It is not easy to make graphological generalizations about such wide ranging and complex psychological categories such as those here above discussed. A few observations might prove to be helpful, though.

Narcissistic grandiosity is often seen in exaggerations of capital letters, enlarged letter height, writing size out of proportion to the space allotted, or unnecessary elaborations that are attention getting. In combination with some degree of rigidity, narrowness and left trending end strokes, it would suggest arrogance, disdain, and unconcern for others. Angles, and threads combined, or signs of neglect of form would indicate a willingness to exploit and

manipulate others for personal gain. Roundedness in narcissistic writing shows an ability to be seductive and more sensitive in knowing how to use people emotionally.
The higher achieving types of narcissists will show signs of simplification, regularity, and average to good spatial organization.

Borderlines tend to have chaotic inner lives with intense emotional turbulence and unpredictable mood swings. This will show in their writing in irregularity of form, sudden change of writing direction, a poorly developed or neglected middle zone, unbalanced zonal distribution, and very often a hastiness or sloppiness in the script.

Irritability and high sensitivity is seen in a weak, changeable downstroke and variable pressure patterns. Uneven baselines reveal a strong mood coloration in their daily activities. Mixed or uneven simplification shows inconsistent use of abilities and achievement potential. Identity problems are expressed in the lowered level of rhythm of form, space, and movement.

Spatial disturbances are an especially strong indicator for social immaturity. A marked tendency toward left trend shows a great deal of self-involvement with a corresponding deficiency of socialization and concern for others.

The schizoidal type is identified by wide spaces between words and/or between letters, strong left trend, narrowness, and signs of reduced emotional expressiveness. This corresponds to the characteristic distancing and withdrawal behaviors of the schizoid.

**Ill #1 Queen Victoria. Age unknown**

Set the tone for the repressive sexuality of her time. Rigid, controlled, angular, no flexibility. Compulsive with strong narcississtic tendencies.

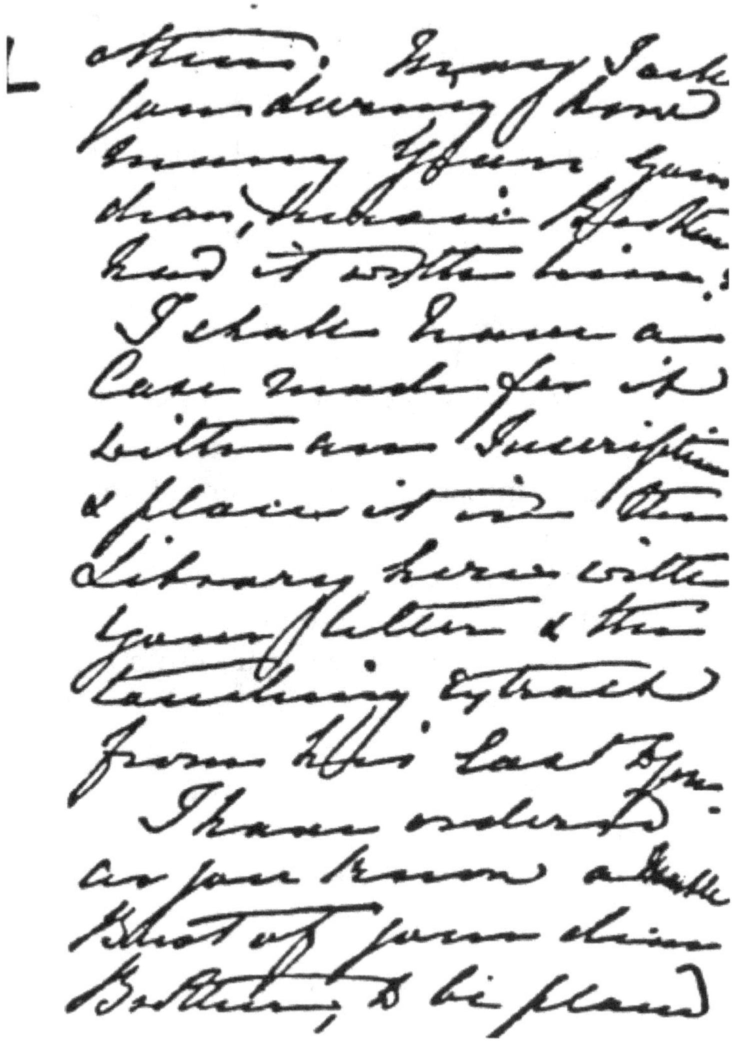

**Ill #2 Napoleon Bonaparte at his zenith**

Grandiosity and need for narcissistic mirroring. Note size of signature and paraph underneath. Great lack of concern for anyone else.

1807.

**Ill #3 Male. Age 50, RH.**

Extremely successful entrepreneur. High intelligence. An exploitative narcissist with mixd features of borderline, schizoid, and paranoid types.

Prod + Cons. +
Import + Export
in each country.
Data sources.
Ind. assns. list.
Regulations in each country.
— inside Ecommerce.

**III #4 Male. Mid 30's. RH. Marketing type**

Successful stockbroker. Angles, thread, and speed suggest the quickly shifting exploiter adjusting to competitive environment ruthlessly.

to be right and quick to
criticise others involved –
a little bit of knowledge
on this aspect of spot month
dealing might have saved

**Ill #5 Male. Age 47. RH**

High-achieving narcissist. Grandiose self-image masks underlying identity confusion. Hard-driving alcoholic.

Roger—

Looking forward

to seeing you again

Marty

P.S. Damien handwriting
Enclosed

**Ill #6 Female. 37. RH**

Seductive narcissist. Needs constant attention and applause. Any failure eleicts rage or depression. Highly impulsive and sef-involved (circular forms).

Dear Roger
I'll be back
on Wed.
I need to
know about
this girl
Love Lynnie

ILL#6

**Ill #7 Female mid-70s. RH**

Narcissistic with ideation that borders on paranoid. Functions well within a very narrow focus. Must avoid ego threats to remain functional.

**III #8 Male. 45. RH**

Borderline. Occaionslly employed opera singer. Chaotic, turbulent, unreliable emotional patterns. Easily irritated. Quickly swings from affection to rage.

Check the Bureau of Birth (For the Bronx I believe it is 1910 ~~Arthur~~ ARTHUR Avenue but not absolutely sure. My address here is c/o Mary Evans 27 Connaught Mansions Prince of Wales drive London S.W. 11

**Ill #9 Female. Age 21. RH.**

Borderline. Alcoholic. Very overweight. Suicidal ideation. Involved in abusive relationship with female partner. Severe problems with femininity and identity.

still in pain but not as much
4/2 went to GYN DR. SAID the same
thing and said to keep taking
my B/C pills. and to come
back on the 14 or 16 of April after
my ultrasound test to see how large
my fibersian tumor is. all this
week having bad hallucinations &

**Ill #10 Male. Age 34. RH.**

Borderline. Was cult follower for six years. Strong clinging and unmet dependency needs. Both passive and aggressive. Works as guidance counselor in urban school system.

---

Dear Beloved,
Love to you in Her
Blessed Name. Praying
for you're inward
& onward journey.
You are dear to me
& am grateful for your
kindness, insight, patience,
& much much
more. May we growth together.
With great love for you
Ram Ram 54
Jeff

**Ill #11 Female. Age 32. RH**

Religious sect member for 10 years. Borderline, struggling to find her own identity. Hard to find suitable work. Very needy and easily depressed.

It was nice talking to you again after so long a time. It has been quite a meaningful year and I'm looking forward to resolving some issues and seeing what the future has to offer.

By the way, I've moved (again) and want

**Ill #12 Male. Mid 30s. RH**

Schizoidal. Works as psychotherapist. High intelligence and awareness but keeps tremendous distance between himself and others. Emotionally remote and unavailable. Note space between words and lines.

---

Thanks Again Terrence—

Be speaking to you +

Enjoy the Holidays

Love

**Ill #13 Male. Age 28. RH**

Schizoid. Successful painter. Original and intelligent but disconnected from his emotions. Peole are used for mirroring and acting out narcissistic illusions.

Ancient energy black cloaked
some may be empty volumes,
jewels, apparitions endless songs
through eternity.

## Bibliography

American Psychiatric Association. *Diagnostic and Statistical Manual of Mental Disorders* (3rd ed.) Washington, D.C. 1980.

Fromm, Erich, *Man for Himself*, Greenwich, Ct: Fawcett Pub. 1947. Lowen, Alexander, Narcissism, New York: MacMillan, 1985.

Masterson, James F., *The Search for the Real Self*, New York: The Free Press, 1988.

Miller, Alice, *The Drama of the Gifted Child*, New York: Basic Books, 1981. Millan, T., Disorders of Personality, New York: Wiley, 1981.

Morrison, A.P., *Essential Papers on Narcissism*, New York: New York University Press, 1986.

Summers, F., *Psychoanalytic Therapy of the Borderline Patient*, Psychoanalytic Psychology, Fall 1988, Pp. 339-355.

# The Lower Zone

# Comments on the Lower Zone

The top of the lower zone is the baseline. It is like the surface of the surface of a body of water. Whatever is below the-surface plane or horizon is the area of the lower zone. Whatever we are not conscious of is found in this zone. Instinctual urges, life force, physical vitality, the id, the unconscious, the elemental self are here.

We do have some degree of conscious contact with this force inside ourselves, and this expression of conscious awareness is also seen in the lower zone, even though it is quite limited in its expression. It is the place for the roots and foundation of the personality. What is placed in this zone and how it fits, whether securely or insecurely, strongly affects the substance and expression of both the middle and upper zones. Essential stability, or lack of it, is seen in the lower zone.

The preference for any zone is seen in emphasis placed on size of forms or emphasis placed on the distinctiveness of forms. Since the LZ is the ground and everything below the ground level it is the source from which the food or basic material of life originates. Hence, materialistic interests and attitudes are most clearly expressed in this area.

The baseline divides the dark from the lighted side of the personality. The LZ is the zone of darkness and also of sleep. Difficulties in falling asleep is seen in uneven pressure in this zone and signs of high levels of sensitivity or nervousness, or difficulties in personal adjustment as seen in all parts of the writing. Life force & vital energy is shown through the pressure. Pressure is the indicator of what the writer feels the senses can offer. Heavy pressure and extension into the LZ shows sensual enjoyment. Almost shows pleasure in eating.

How well the writer can assimilate what is found in the LZ is seen in how well the loops are formed and how the movement is brought back into the middle zone of reality. Realization of physical pleasure is seen in how well the writer behaves graphically in the LZ.

Do the forms serve the purpose for which they are intended in dipping into this zone. If the writer stays for too short a time he is not getting enough LZ energy. If he stays for too long a visit he is not efficient is satisfying his needs, which will cause frustrations. LZ difficulties, restated, are basically, the writer doesn't know what to do once he gets there and cannot tap his life force sufficiently; or, the writer dips his bucket into the well but doesn't know how to get it back into the daylight—of consciousness like going into a dark cellar and not finding the way up again.

#### The extensions into the LZ

These should normally be completed with a loop that completes the form and returns the energy to the middle zone, Many writers make the downstroke only, eliminating the loop. The analyst must determine whether this is simplification of form or neglect of form. If it occurs only at the end of words it is simplification and shows a sense of efficiency. If the pressure on the downstroke fades after the baseline it indicates that there is weakened desire to descend or the writer feels too insecure in going down into this zone. If the downstroke shows a hook added it shows a lack of release, aggression, and imbalance.

When the loops are malformed, for instance, turning to the right instead of to the left, it shows an inversion of direction, a reaching for the father in the wrong way which causes the stroke to be completed toward the left or the mother, and is a strong indicator of sexual confusion and/or deviation.

If in the same writing the loops close 1) too high 2) too low 3) properly on the base line, the explanation is l) the person was originally shy and closed off. 2) became unfulfilled as a result 3) gradually learned to achieve the proper integration of LZ energy.

When the writer has pressure in his script and then at some time in his life loses it, this shows sickness and loss of vital energy either real or imagined in the writer's mind.

## The lowercase letter 'F' and the daily routines

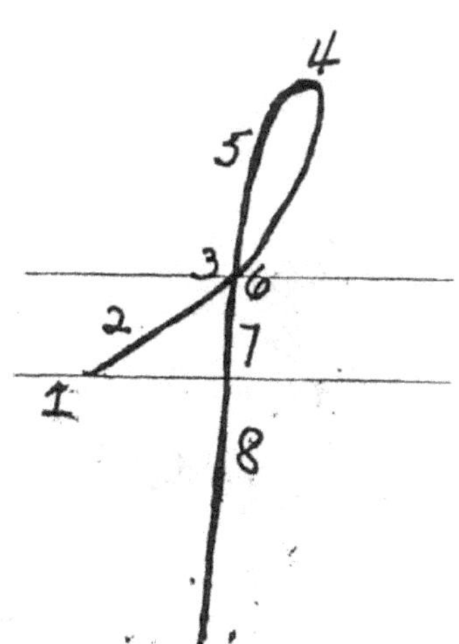


1. Sunrise
2. Daily routine after wakening
3. Start to work
4. Lunch or midday
5. Afternoon
6. Return home
7. Evening routine 8, Go to sleep

**Ed Koch, Mayor of New York**

When I was 17, I wanted to look like a preppy, even though I wasn't attending a preppy school. And, I also had hair when I was 17. Today I still like to dress informally, although my hairline has changed.

Ed Koch

**Exploiter**

the sophistication and
urbanity which are an [illegible]
part of your being. I of[illegible]
think of the way you des[illegible]
the balance sheet of your
past relationships and I
wonder if I have enough
offer you to keep those
[illegible] between you and me.
affection for you is so
profound, I feel inspired
to reach to the very depths
of myself to find gifts to
bring to you. I know, I
[illegible] and you
probably already under-
stand that underlying
insecurity. Anyway,
I miss you constantly
Love, Kandu

**Exploiter**

You gave me a lot of substance to think about--mainly inquiring into my own feelings. Unfamiliar territory, but should be interesting.

Three samples of Mr. Hinckley's handwriting are stapled together. The envelope arrived today-- after my having discussed, tentatively, a partnership arrangement. The other two are much earlier.

Also enclosed is a sample of Kandy's hand-- so big and round.

I shall return from Mexico the 27th. May I call you then?

Allen Bragdon

**Male - 22- RH.** Country Western singer; was a coke addict, then turned to Coca Cola, etc.

Well, here's what
I ate for breakfast:
I had a little shakti
and a lot
of Love and
some Coca Cola
and fresh air.
Bruce Hall King

Dan Quayle, U.S. Vice-President

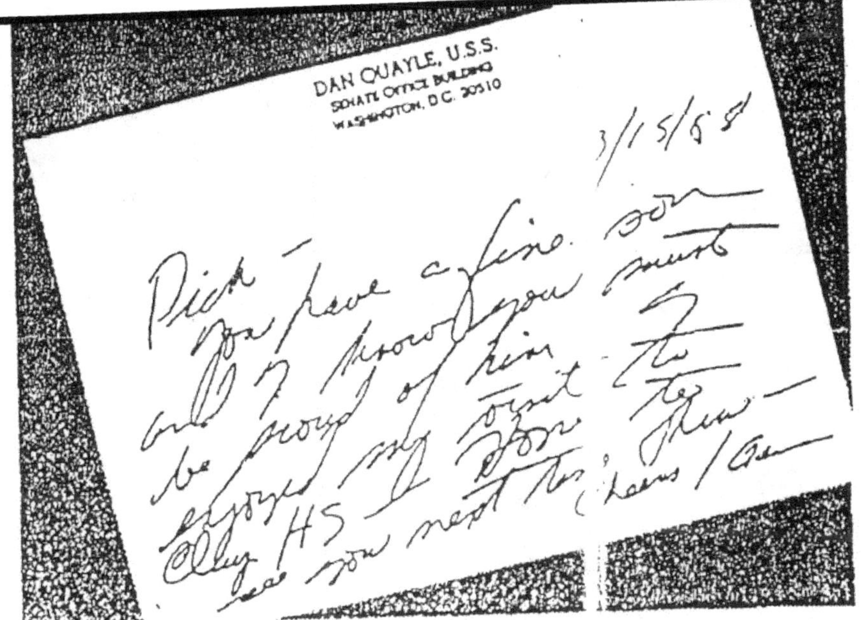

DAN QUAYLE, U.S.S.
SENATE OFFICE BUILDING
WASHINGTON, D.C. 20510

3/15/88

Rick –
You have a fine son
and I know you must
be proud of him. I
enjoyed my visit to the
Clay HS. I hope to
see you next time. Cheers / Dan

**F - 35 -** Study to be a theologian and a psychic. A "serial rebeller." Says she's never been in love. May have been sexually abused.

I had my first day of school today
nd it went OK. I think my classes will be
teresting. So I forgot what I was going to say
Now I remember; psychologists analyze patient
wings of drawings of their parents. My favorite
is pink and I really love to babysit.

That's it

I'm outta here

Nice meeting you

Vandi

Roger Rubin

**F-40 -** PhD psychotherapist. Had a child just prior to writing this.

October 15

Dear Lynn,

We had planned to have a session several weeks ago. I hope everything is going well for you. Please call when you want to set up the session.

Best wishes,

Julie

F/40

M-55. Very heavy pressure

Divorced in 1985, after 20 years of a duty-driven, dysfunctional marriage, I will be suffering the financial burden of a relatively generous alimony agreement until 1995. My son, Brian, who means more to me than anyone or anything else, should graduate from Amherst College next June, and is preparing applications to the best medical schools in the country.

Socially, people, particularly women, are responding and reaching out to me more openly than ever in the past. My comfort levels with women have improved a lot in the last few years. My uncertainty about the viability of my career and future prospects, however, is making it very difficult for me to maintain stable and mutually satisfying relationships.

The curious thing is that my efforts to deal with the future are increasingly focusing on preparing and positioning myself to help other people do effective life and career planning. It interests and attracts me greatly, but I am not sure it is well directed energy. Am I coping with or avoiding reality.

Mother

Last week in Hornell - the girl with whom I'd roomed at the Heights before we were married - lost her husband with a heart attack. He'd worked for the telephone Co. but had retired. He had physicals regularly & thot himself in perfect condition. He was about 10 yrs. older than us. - He'd been out all day & died in his sleep as he took a quick nap before dinner. While we sent flowers, we feel badly that we couldn't go over.

All in all it was quite a week!

Yesterday Betty called to bring me up to date on the Barshet's doings. She said "Guess what!" ~~Betty~~ Becky had not secured a job in Rochester as she'd hoped so is home and taking grad. course at Elmira College. But up at Rochester she'd met a grad student from India and had dated [illegible]m. When she moved home he made the necessary inquiries & had been down in Elmira for the weekend and they'd gone out of course. She said Ed doesn't know what [illegible]
very da[illegible]

[illegible]larly & thot himself in perfect conditi[illegible]
older than us. - He'd been out all day &
took a quick nap before dinner. Whi[illegible]
feel badly that we couldn't go over.
[illegible] all it was quite a week!
[illegible] Betty called to bring me up to date on th[illegible]
[illegible]ess what!" ~~Betty~~ Becky had not secured a job
[illegible] is home and taking grad. course at Elm[illegible]
[illegible] she'd met a grad [illegible]

**Father**

Monday July 14

Dear Sharon and Charles

The top of my head is very red from sunburn and my face is very red because it has taken me so long, as we used to say to take my pen in hand and reply to your last letter. Its been so long, in fact, that I hardly know where to start. We've talked several times, which also confuses the issue of what has been covered. Anyway —

The Fourth was spent in the back yard, weeding and the like, which was where I got the second dose of red-head. (the first was at the cemetery in Rochester on June 28th) Saturday morning we drove to Henrietta, because it was time to see Pop and because Paul was there. P., C. and L. went over to see Pop in the afternoon. Found him in fair spirits and health, ~~but~~ except for his memory which worries him more (restaurant)

**Charles' girlfriend**

Chuck —

I miss saying "good night" to you - it felt good to end the day with you -

On the Dracula paper — he said "you write pretty well but -" and went on to criticize the way I used quotes but I was so thankful for the — "pretty well" - at least I'm in the ball park.

Kathleen came over today and tie-dyed T-shirts with me. It was so good to see her. She's picking up Kristy's car. She said Kristy's trying Wishing you a very Happy Birthday to stop smoking. They had a good talk -

Jimmy & I are looking forward to Saturday, I always love the first moment of seeing you again. & thereafter. Love J.

**Charles' second girlfriend.** Social worker, known each other a short time and she wants a commitment.

3:30 AM Tuesday 6/4/91

Dear Chuck:

I have done another of my early morning awakenings & cannot seem to go back to sleep. It would bother me exc[ept] that some of my best thinking happens.

I need to call you tonight. But a couple of things can be written as well.

Re how I spend money – you asked – you know the biggest single item outside rent is Elaine – 85.00 a (weekly) throw. Actually I get reimbursed 40% of her fee. I collect it about every 6 months & put the reimbursement in my Dreyfus account. Dreyfus is somewhere between checking account & retirement. It's what I pay huge bills out of & buy a car from. Anyway, I could undoubtedly trim every thing I spend a little (except clothes – I don't buy too many clothes!) gifts, books, lunches/dinners out, food, (professional expenses) phone ... I could probably trim it all. (I was doing end/beginning of the month figuring tonight)

You surprised me Sat.. You have never led me to believe you wanted me on your territory so it would not occur to me to invite myself to your house. Good grief – there are some vestiges of a

# The Uses and Abuses of Insecurity

## A graphological perspective

# Uses and Abuses of Insecurity

Before discussing some of the effects and results of insecurity, I think it would be helpful to establish a base line idea of what creates security.

A. **Symbiotic or dual union**. First and foremost, this must be established during the child's first 15 months. The child needs a face with accepting eyes to reflect and mirror his self back to him. Whatever is in the nurturing person's eyes becomes the core and foundation of the child's identity.

B. **Getting narcissistic needs met**. Physical and emotional needs are not thwarted or frustrated but, instead, satisfied, and gratified.

C. **Warm contact**. If we can feel the caring touch and warmth from an emotionally available person we can establish a sense of trust. We can believe the world is friendly and warm and can depend on out there to get our needs met.

D. **The need for autonomy**. We need the opportunity to differentiate ourselves from our parents. Starting from about 15 — 18 months, children begin the process of separation and individuation. Only after a successful bonding can we make a successful separation. This the first of a lifetime of going off on our own.

E. **A dependable and predictable environment**. Children need reliable parents to count on as they begin to test their personal limits and create their own identity. They need to discover and trust in safe and stable boundaries.

F. **Experiencing pleasure**. Everyone needs age-appropriate fun and stimulation at every stage of development.

G. **Experience legitimate pain**. Legitimate pain and suffering allow us to learn from experience in a healthy way.

H. **Dependency needs met**. The belief that one's needs will be met in a reasonably predictable manner. In other words, a mother and father (or other caregiver) with a firm identity who can be relied on to be there.

Getting these security needs met allows us to establish self-value, self-esteem, and an underlying sense of worthiness, and is the basis for achieving any degree of self-actualization. It is also the basis for self-love and self-acceptance. It is the foundation for happiness and the love of others.

John Bradshaw, who is quoted and paraphrased extensively for this paper, as well as Alice Miller, Gershen, Kaufman and others, believe that the basic core of what we experience as insecurity comes from the feeling of shame which when carried to an extreme becomes "toxic" and dehumanizing.

Kaufman writes, "Shame is the affect which is the source of many complex and disturbing inner states: depression, alienation, self-doubt, isolating loneliness, paranoid and schizoid phenomena, compulsive disorders, splitting of the self, perfectionism, a deep sense of inferiority, inadequacy or failure, the so-called borderline conditions, and disorders of narcissism. (Shame: the Power of Caring)

A few comments about healthy shame and unhealthy shame might be useful. Healthy shame lets us know that we are limited. We are not omnipotent and grandiose in our beings or in our power. Limitation is our essential nature and it is okay to entertain some level of self-doubt. According to Erik Erikson, a sense of shame is part of the second stage of psychosocial development.

The first stage is the child needs to develop a sense of basic trust. This is done through our primary caretakers. They need to be predictable, mirroring, comforting and trustworthy. It is in the second stage, from about 15 months to three years that the child begins to develop autonomy and starts testing the limits of the world around him and begins to discover his limits. It is in this process that healthy doubt and shame are developed. This creates the feeling of core boundaries and limitedness which never allows us to believe we it all. Also, at this time shyness occurs which as a healthy feeling of shame is a reluctance to expose oneself. The basis for blushing also is established here. Blushing results from being caught off guard unexpectedly and feeling a degree of healthy shame.

Unhealthy or toxic shame Bradshaw calls "the shame that binds you" is experienced as the all pervasive sense that one is flawed and defective as a human being. "Toxic shame is no longer an emotion that signal our limits, it is a state of being, a core identity. Toxic share gives one a sense of worthlessness, a sense of failing, a falling short as a human.

Toxic shame is a rupture of the self with the self." It is experienced as an inner torment, a sickness of the soul. Merle Fossom and Marilyn Mason in their book Facing Shame: *Families in Recovery describe it this way*:

Same is an inner sense of being completely diminished or insufficient as a person. It is the self-judging the self. A moment of share my be humiliation so painful or an indignity so profound, that one feels one has been robbed of his or her dignity, or exposed as inadequate, bad, or worthy of rejection. A pervasive sense of shame is the ongoing premise that one is fundamentally bad, inadequate, defective, unworthy, or not fully valid as a human being.

At this point, it would be useful to contrast shame with guilt so the difference between the is better understood. Healthy guilt is the emotional core of our conscience. It is emotion which results from behaving in a manner contrary to our beliefs and values. According to Erikson, the Third stage of psychosocial development is the polar balance between initiative and guilt. Guilt presupposes internalized rules and develops later than shame. Developmentally it is more mature than shame. Fossum and Mason write that

"While guilt is a painful feeling of regret and responsibility for one's actions, shame is a painful feeling about oneself as a person. The possibility for repair seems foreclosed to the shameful person because shame is a matter of identity... not of behavioral infraction."

Any human emotion can be internalized. When internalized, an emotion stops functioning in the manner of an emotion and becomes a characterological style, the core of the person's character, his identity. In the case of shame, internalization is the result of identification with unreliable and shame-based models and the trauma of abandonment which binds feelings, needs, and drives with shame.

**Parents abandon children in the following ways**

- By actually physically leaving them
- By not being there to affirm their children's expression of emotion

- By not providing for their children's developmental dependency needs
- By physically, sexually, emotionally abusing them
- By using children to take care of their own unmet dependency needs
- By using children to take care of their marriages
- By hiding and denying their shame secrets to the outside world so that the children have to protect these covert issues in order to keep the family balance
- By not giving them their time, attention, and direction
- By acting shameless

The job of parents is to model behaviors for their children to follow. Modeling includes how to be a man or woman; how to relate intimately to another person; how to acknowledge and express emotions; how to have physical, emotional, and intellectual boundaries; how to cope with life's problems; how to be self-disciplined; how to love oneself and others. Dysfunctional parents can't do these well or at all. Many don't how. They themselves were children of dysfunctional families and were deeply wounded or deprived. It has been observed that 96% of all American families are dysfunctional to a greater or lesser degree. Although unprovable and startling, it is likely to be true. The level of dysfunctional behavior around us is extraordinarily high and pervasive.

### Shame as Alienation

Dysfunctional parents produce dysfunctional children. Children cannot know they are without good reflective mirrors. When mirroring is defective they experience abandonment. This is also caused by neglect of developmental dependency needs or abuse of any kind. One of the most common results is a sense of alienation. Alienation means that one experiences parts of oneself as separate, apart and disconnected from the self. As an example, if you were never allowed to express anger in your family, your anger becomes an alienated part of yourself. You experience toxic shame when you feel angry. This part of you must be disowned or severed. The condition of inner alienation and isolation is accompanied by a low grade chronic depression. This has to do with the sadness of losing one's authentic self. This also applies to the expression of sexual feelings, sorrow, being afraid and of feeling joy.

### Shame as the False Self

Exposure of the self to self lies at the heart of neurotic share, so escape from the self is necessary. This is accomplished by creating a false self. This false self is always more or less than human. It could a perfectionist or a slob, a family hero or family scapegoat. Layers of defense and pretense are so intense that one loses awareness of who one really is.

Whether the role chosen is that of a super achieving perfectionist or an addict in an alley, the core motivation is the neurotic shame that drives them to assume family roles and life roles that reflect a deep sense of self rupture. To name but a few of the many roles children play in dysfunctional families: hero, little parent, spouse, victim, caretaker, saint, athlete, peacemaker, scapegoat, the perfect one, the problem, the rebel , lost child, achiever. These roles allow one to survive and feel a sense of control and protection.

### Shame as Codependency

As Bradshaw uses the concept, codependency is a loss of one's inner reality and an addiction to outer reality. As part of the abandonment process a child gives up his own reality in order to take care of the parent(s) or the needs of the family system. The child survives by the defense of not being there. It is easiest to see co-dependence in the activity addictions such as alcohol or drug addiction. Co-dependents try to make themselves indispensable by taking care of others, by enabling them to continue the addiction. They are willing to do whatever it takes to be loved or worthwhile.

### Shame as the Core of Compulsive/Addictive Behaviors

Our society seems to be in serious trouble. Twenty-five percent of the population is either alcoholic or addicted to other drugs. This is a conservative figure which does not include nicotine or caffeine. There may be as many as 60 million sexual abuse victims. Some claim that as many as one in eight women are battered. Eating disorders are rampant. Workaholism is a widespread condition.

Bradshaw defines compulsive/addictive behavior as "a pathological relationship to any mood altering experience that has life damaging consequences." Another one is "any process used to avoid or take away intolerable reality." Because it takes away intolerable pain it becomes our highest priority and takes time and energy from other parts of our life thus, its life damaging consequences. The intolerable pain it takes away is the shame based feeling of utter aloneness, grief, and sense of being flayed to one's core. Shame begets shame. The more one seeks solace the more one becomes ashamed of the very seeking of it. Alcohol, sleeping pills, and tranquilizers are depressants, and numb feelings. Stimulants such as cocaine, hallucinogens, nicotine, and caffeine create an artificial strength, freedom, and control.

Food addictions are divided into four categories: obesity, anorexia nervosa, bulimia and the fat/thin disorder. It is estimated that at least 34 million people are obese, 60% of them women. Obese people are shame-bound in either their angry or sad feelings. They feel empty and lonely, and eat to be filled or full in order to numb their painful underlying emotions.

Anorexics take control of the family with their starving and weight loss. They are rigidly controlled, deny all feelings, especially sexuality, are super-achieving and live behind a wall of pretense. They renounce their emotions by refusing to eat. In bulimia the bingeing cycle intensifies the underlying shame which then triggers the purge cycle and adds self disgust and self contempt. Vomiting is a way to cleanse themselves of the shameful amount of food they just devoured. In the fat/thin disorder, by constantly thinking about eating or not eating one is distracted from real feelings.

Bradshaw mentions feeling addictions whereby an undesirable feeling is replaced by what was a family-authorized feeling. The most common addiction to an emotion is that form of intensified anger called rage. Rage is the only emotion that can't be controlled by shame. When we are raging, we feel unified within, no longer split, no longer inadequate and defective. We are mood-altered. Other feeling addictions are addiction to sadness, fear, excitement, religious righteousness, even to guilt, which keeps one working endlessly on oneself analyzing every event and transaction ad infinitum.

Activity addictions are buying, hoarding, sexing, reading, gambling, exercising, watching sports, watching TV, and caring for pets. The addiction to work allows the workaholic to avoid painful feelings of loneliness, inadequacy, and depression.

## Defenses against Shame

There are many defenses against deep shame such as the primary ego defense of denial which is the attempt to deny the hurt that is going on. Fantasy bonding, which is clinging to the illusion that there is somebody there who loves one, which is a way of clinging to the abuser. Repression is used to numb out feelings.

### Dissociation

This is the defense that splits one from the fomenting reality by substituting another for it at the same time. This is often seen in cases of severe sexual or physical abuse, and is the basis of the split personality syndrome. There are others as well, such as projection, somatic conversions, and reaction formations. A more complex defense against toxic shame is to act shameless. This is a strategy which becomes a characterological style.

### Perfectionism

Perfectionism is learned when one is valued only for doing and perfuming, and this is the basis for love. Kaufman writes, "When perfectionism is paramount, the comparison of self with others inevitably ends in the self-feeling the lesser for the consequence. Comparing and judging lead to a destructive kind of competitiveness which aims at outdoing others and being one up on them, rather than being the best one can be"

### Striving for power and control

Power is a form of control and those who must control everything feel vulnerable to being shamed, being exposed so that it can be seen that they are flawed and defective. They need to be higher on the pecking order to feel adequate and superior. Only by having power over others can one reverse the role of early childhood. It is a reenactment of their original victimization. Control means attempting to limit other people's thoughts, feelings, and actions. It destroys intimacy and equality. In its most neurotic form, it is and out and out addiction. Individuals spend all their energies planning and scheming for position in order to climb the ladder of success.

**Criticism and blame**

These are perhaps the most common ways that shame is transferred interpersonally. If one feels put down and humiliated, then one can reduce this feeling by blaming and criticizing someone else. When your mother says, "You never think of anyone but yourself," you are likely to feel deeply shamed, and grow up to do the same to those around you.

Caretaking and helping are activities that distract one from feelings of inadequacy. This occurs when the goal of the caretaker is the caretaking and not the good of the person being cared for. This leads to enabling or rescuing and is characteristic of codependency. Parents often enable or rescue their children, doing for them what they could not do for themselves. The children wind up feeling inadequate or defective.

People pleasing and being 'nice' is a to avoid any real emotional intimacy and contact. By avoiding intimacy, the people pleaser makes sure that no one sees him as he really is with feelings of shame and inadequacy. This behavior is characteristic of Pollyannas, religiously righteous people, and those who are behaving in a compulsively positive manner.

Bradshaw says that to heal our toxic shame we must come out of hiding. As long as our shame is hidden there is nothing we can do about it. In order to change it, we must embrace it. The only way out is through. The last half of Healing the Shame that Binds You is devoted to ideas and methods for externalizing the internalized shame that most of us carry around. He believes very much in using groups, especially those that use the 12 Step program originated in Alcoholics Anonymous, as well as in intensive personal work.

Illustrations with histories follow.

Ill#1 Female. 50. Right hand. Successful artist, wife, and mother. Well adjusted, nurturing and creative personality. Conventional, yet expressively original. Positive, healthy symbiotic union. As a result, is well integrated and balanced.

Dear Mr. Rubin –

Having thought about what these two paragraphs would (should) say for the past few days, naturally I've waited until the last possible moment before catching a plane to Washington to write. This of course means that I'm in a frantic rush and not being especially careful.

Ill#2 Female. 75. Right hand. Very successful psychiatrist with strong interest in aesthetics. Mature, developed personality. Balance between intellectual and emotional areas. Brought up by a cold mother but a loving nanny and loving father. Good early security pattern. Form and space rhythms are strong.

I know that this is wrong.
but I feel that I am slipping
badly and that I better stop
now to try too much before I will
be forced to do it.
I wish I had my old self-
confidence So please tell me

Ill#3 Male. 65. Right hand. Retired psychiatrist, art and antique collector. Superior analytic intelligence. Emotionally detached, controlled, irritable. Narcissistic needs thwarted and frustrated. Extreme angularity suggests hostility, independence and defiance to father and authority.

6/27/84

Dear Ms. von Zweck—

I regret that Jessie gave you my name without consulting me. If she had told me her intentions, I would have flagged her down.

I have lived here some 11 years, and at first liked it. For the past 3 or 4 years I have soured on the place completely, and, when I can get my affairs & possessions organized, I plan to move to Virginia. As a matter of fact, I will be busy doing just that, and may actually be on my way when you arrive here in September.

e had told me her intentions, I would have

have lived here some 11 years, and at first

ast 3 or 4 years I have soured on the plac

. I can get my affairs & possessions orga

ve to Virginia. As a matter of fact, I wi

Ill. #4 Male. 46. Right hand. High-powered investment banker. Narcissistically deprived. Overcontrolled as child. Toilet trained age 12 months. Parents were intellectual, cool, and avoided touching him. Competitive, aggressive, and intelligently exploitative. High level of tension and poor release pattern.

I am writing to ask you to analyze my handwriting from the sample I am writing now and from a previous 1977/78 sample I dug out at random; and, finally, I include a recent letter from my father to my wife which will provide the requested sample of his handwriting.

I could not come up with a sample of my mother's script, nor could I find any from college days of my own.

While I am interested in any comments

Ill. #5 Female. 32. Right hand. Jewelry designer and crafts artist. Moderately successful but working below her capacity. High intelligence and awareness levels, emotionally underdeveloped. Little warmth and touching from mother, resulting in feelings of rejection and deep self-doubt. Unresolved identity issues interferes with being fully productive. Feels flawed and isolated.

more - expensive, and finely finished woven patterns from Europe, and offer many novelty cloths and printed ribbons to our customers.

Our largest customer base is florists, followed by craft accounts. The gift trade, which most consumers commonly associate our product with is our least profitable market.

Hope this little piece on

Ill. #6 Male. 60's. Right hand. Father of Fig. #5. He is emotionally unavailable to himself and others. Main motivation and activity is directed to success in the business world.

#6

Alice —
I hope you find this useful
in your quest for identity
Love
Dad

#7

Ill. #7 Female. 50's. Mother of Fig. #5. Became psychotherapist in later life. Cool, detached, controlled. High intelligence but emotionally withholding.

Dear Alice,
I hope that you not only find
the right answers, but discover the
right questions —
Love
Mom

ILL. #8 Female. Mid 40's. Right hand. Successful primal therapist. Narrowness, wide word spacing and high upper zone/long lower zone indicate repression, inhibition, and fearlessness. Strong tension and weak release cause anger and frustration. Mother was critical, rigid, and impossible to please, a guilt dispenser. This writer has an overdeveloped superego, weak ego, and is guilt-ridden. She tends to blame others for her problems.

*Kimberley, B.C. is situated about 200 miles north of Spokane, Washington*
*It is near Trail, B.C, Fernie, B.C, Nelson, B.C, Kelowna, B.C*
*I attended twelve years of school there and then went to the*
*University of British Columbia which is in Vancouver, B.C, 700 miles away*
*Married my highschool boy friend at age 21, had Pamela at age*
*24, Scott 17 months later, lost one baby at age 29 and that*
*is why I adopted Darryl. My husband and I divorced after*
*11 years of marriage. Three years later I re-married James who is*
*9 years younger. That ended in a separation 7 months ago because*
*of various conflicts. His handwriting is included.*
*I now live in New York City with Pamela and Darryl, Scott*
*lives with his father in Canada. I have been in New York*
*three years and feel happy about my decision to stay here after*
*James and I split. I like to jog, dance, read and listen to*
*music. My writing has changed alot in the past 10 years and*
*even more since a teenager. I remember feeling bad about*
*my first writing. It was like this Jan Scott Ure*

Ill. #9 Male 46. Right hand. Was a ranking police officer, now a lawyer and a writer. Both parents alcoholic resulting in severe early abandonment problems for him. he is currently dealing effectively with his own substance abuse issues. His somewhat chaotic inner life leads to instability in emotional relationships.

I want to see you because I believe this to be a moment of ~~transition~~ in my life, of roads to be taken and not taken. Maybe there are answers in the

There are answers in one's handwriting, no doubt, but to read them is the problem. Therefore, I come to you now for guidance, a reading, an insight, or maybe no more than a hint. In any case, help. I enclose an [illegible] document with [illegible]

Ill. #10 Male. 42. Right hand. Successful documentary film maker. Poor parenting resulted in severe emotional alienation and distancing. Very intelligent and creative but emotionally underdeveloped.

Here is what I have of this
handwriting. Here is my own too,
for that matter!
I have a couple of very nice
lady friends who are looking for
someone nice - perhaps we might
have dinner sometime when I get
back from St. Thomas (I am off
to a film festival wed - sunday

writing. Here is my own
that matter!
I have a couple of very
friends who are looking
one nice - perhaps we
dinner sometime when
from St. Thomas (I

ILL. #11 Male. 49. Left hand. Very successful business executive. Emotionally deprived and poorly nurtured as child. Feelings are detached and out of touch. He is a driven workaholic, absorbing high levels of tension and stress.

You had asked how the fact that DLJ can delay placing the business with us can cause us problems because we would be paying out to brokers under the min. provision of their contracts. This is handled in the agreement by restricting to 100,000 contracts the amount they can delay or we are assured of getting 300,000 contracts during the 6 month period and this amount of business should keep us from having problem with the min provision of the contracts. Contracts in this manner mean outright

## BIBLIOGRAPHY

Bradshaw, John. Bradshaw. *On The Family.* Deerfield Beach, FL Health

Bradshaw, John. *Healing the Shame that Bind You.* Deerfield Beach, FL Health

Erikson, Erik. *Childhood and Society.* New York: W.W. Norton.

Fossum, M. and Mason, M. *Facing Shame.* New York: W.W. Norton.

Kaufman, Gershen. *Shame: The power of Caring.* MASS: Schenkman Books.

Miller, Alice. *The Drama of the Gifted Child.* New York: Basic

Satir, Virginia. *Conjoint Family Therapy.* Alto, CA: Science and Behavior.

# Signs of Dishonesty in Handwriting

Roger Rubin

# Notes from a 1993 Workshop

INITIAL CONSIDERATIONS: It is essential to keep in mind that no single indicator is sufficient to allow an interpretation of either insincerity or dishonesty. Four or more indicators must be present and the "Gestalt," or the overall configuration of the writing, must confirm this before the writer can be judged as lacking in sincerity or honesty.

The Graphologist cannot predict the kind of circumstances that would have to prevail in order to trigger dishonest actions. It is, however, possible to caution involved persons, provided that a detailed description of the job or circumstances is made available. The greatest care should be taken so that a person' s reputation or chances for a job are not damaged due to faulty judgment.

It must be kept in mind that the opinion of just what constitutes dishonesty varies considerably. The handwriting evaluator has to make it quite clear to what degree a writer might be dishonest. Another factor to be considered whenever possible is that the ethics of a person can vary as a result of the combinations of social groups that play a role in one's life, such as ethnic affiliation, nationality, profession, income classes, etc.

Morality, in this context, is relative to the ethics and values embedded in the social contract of the group to which one belongs.

**COVER STROKES**: These are downstrokes that are covered by upstrokes in the middle and lower zones, and are reversed in the upper zone where the upstroke is covered by a downstroke. The downstroke is a symbol of inner security while the upstroke symbolizes the link to the "you" and the world around us. Covering up the connection to the outside world implies an intention to hide. Cover strokes symbolize the shadows or the avoidance of light.

Cover strokes are not primary indicators of dishonesty. However, they do create the psychological environment in which dishonesty can flourish.

Unnecessary circular movement in the middle zone may cause cover strokes in the curves. This movement must be seen as a symbolic repetition of the protective spinning around oneself by a cocoon. It is a clear indicator of insecurity, of reluctance to let the outside world see what is going on within the writer.

Another symbolic comparison could be the retreat of a snail into the shell when the snail feels threatened. The retreat of the writer into the very center of the writing surely implies the same meaning, feeling threatened and hiding. "The world should not be aware of my insecurity; I must do whatever is necessary to prevent anybody seeing me that way."

**COVER STROKES IN THE UPPER ZONE** show inhibition, hiding of ideas, plans, intentions, and also a kind of self-denial (Pulver).

**COVER STROKES IN THE MIDDLE ZONE** indicate hiding of real feelings, deception in the way one feels and behaves in a social setting or what others can see in one. According to Pulver, the cover strokes in the middle zone indicate deceit in the emotional sphere and sometimes business cunning.

**COVER STROKES IN THE LOWER ZONE** indicate deception and hiding of material and sexual concern. Instinctual concealment (Pulver).

**SLOWNESS**: This often should not be regarded as a sign of dishonesty, but it is very often found that criminals write very slowly. Slowness represents reduction of spontaneity and thereby gives time to premeditate, calculate or create circumstances that can lead to acts of dishonesty.

**THREAD**: primary thread (with pressure and relatively slower) is not a thread of convenience but a thread of choice. It should be evaluated as a form of simplification and not as a neglect of form, which would indicate that the person writing primary thread is doing it for the sake of showing, through the simplification, his efficiency and ease of form; in other words, something very favorable.

**SECONDARY THREAD**: can be characterized as a thread without pressure and truly represents neglect of form. If this occurs primarily at the end of words, it is less indicative of insincerity. However, in the middle of a word, the secondary thread is a strong indication of insincerity.

An exception to this could be found in a handwriting that does not show any pressure in the result of the writing. It must be assumed that the lack of pressure in the thread is one criterion governing the whole writing.

Extensive thread formation of the writing shows weak personal values, little self-respect, possibly avoidance of reality, opportunism, slyness, willingness to adjust to different influences, combined with a low level of value discrimination. Also, inner restraints are weak. Pulver's interpretation of thready connection lists (a) adaptation at any cost; (b) high intellectual skills, great psychic flexibility, possible use of understanding people to deceive them. And, are most significant when threads appear within words: (c) a wavering line is an extended thread form with the interpretation of undependability, not keeping promises, no firm goals, lying through deeds rather than words.

**ARCADES:** The high arcade is strongly form-connected and should not be regarded as a sign of insincerity. The creeping arcade, also called the shallow arcade, shows a neglect of the arcade form, and emphasizes the tendency to hide and pretend, or act in an insincere manner.
The shallow or low arcade is the trademark of the conman and the swindler, and signifies pretension, scheming, and lack of principles.

**TERMINAL ARCADES** (bent to the left) show lack of spontaneity and are an expression of calculation, cautiousness, dishonesty, and brutality if done with heavy pressure.

**LETTERS OPEN ON THE BOTTOM**: Here we are talking about middle zone letters, mostly a's and o's. The requirement is a malformation of the letter which would turn into a shallow arcade, indicating inversion of values. The openness on the bottom would allow an overemphasis of influence from the lower zone to such an extent that it must be considered improper and unexpected. The inversion of the movement clearly indicates a hiding tendency and truly equates with disturbed values and a strong indication of dishonesty.

**ARTIFICIAL WRITING**: Strong emphasis on persona or the way one wants to appear to others indicates: lack of naturalness, insincerity, artificial mannerisms and hypocrisy.

**EXTREMES IN WRITING**: Some are: extreme penetration into the lower zone, interference between middle and upper zone, horizontal interference between letters, disturbed movement, form, or space with indicates confusion of values, lack of balance in the writer's value system.

**CURLING**: Roll-ins, claw strokes, terminal letters ending with arcade strokes reaching below the base line, *Sacre Coeur* hooks, smearing, knotted letters all indicate deceit, vanity, guilt, immaturity, and self-involvement.

**SIGNATURE DIFFERENT THAN TEXT**: Appears different from true identity, pretense, hiding.

**EXTREME LEFT TREND**: Preoccupied with self; does not share common values.

**WIDE UNEVEN SPACES IN HIGH FORM LEVEL**: Trickiness, deceit, manipulative.

**DIRECTIONAL PRESSURE FROM ABOVE** into lower zone: Show anxiety about material values which can ultimately lead to dishonesty.

**TOUCHING UP OF LETTERS WITHOUT IMPROVEMENT OF LEGIBILITY**: (Saudek, Pulver) Insincerity to dishonesty, hiding one's intentions.

**CAPITAL LETTERS IN THE MIDDLE OF WORDS**: Confusion of values, insincerity, emphasis wrongly placed.

**EXTREME RIGHT SLANT AND IMPULSIVENESS**: Must have own way, no restraint, as seen in the Hitler writing.

**EXTREME ILLEGIBILITY**: This indicates the writer does not want to be seen as he is; hides; does not want to communicate.

**PRIMITIVENESS OF FORM**: Ordinarily could not be a lack of writing agility or low intelligence which, in itself, is not a sign of dishonesty. However, it does show poor ability to discriminate and is frequently found in the script of criminals.

**DOUBLE IMPULSES IN SINGLE LETTERS**: Ordinarily a sign of insecurity but can develop into dishonesty.

**EXTREME RIGIDITY OR EXTREME SLACKNESS**: The rigid writer ‘cracks’ when confronted with change, or will do anything to protect his fixed structure. The slack writer yields too readily when confronted with a criminal impulse and cannot maintain any stable value structure.

## FOUR CLASSIFICATIONS OF DISHONESTY

**Dishonesty Type #1** — Motive to lie and conceal based on Self-Protection: Distrust, Suspicion, Egotism, Conceit, Self-Love, Self-Esteem, Pride, Arrogance, Vanity

**Dishonesty Type #2** — Motive to lie and conceal based on Inferiority Feelings: Lack of Self-Assurance, Inferiority Feelings, Insecurity relative to others, Timidness, shyness, fear of repercussion or retaliation, white lie, diplomacy lie. Afraid to open one’s mouth and speak up. To maintain a mask, to hide behind Appeasement in situations one does not really like or is opposed to; cowardice.

**Dishonesty Type #3** — Motive to lie and conceal based on self-aggrandizement: Capricious invention (Fisherman’s Stories), passing off fiction as truth, Illusions, Daydreams, braggadocio, Passing off half-knowledge for expertise.

**Dishonesty Type #4** — Motive to lie and conceal based on self-gain and Planned Advantage: To manipulate others for personal gain, Sting-Lie (Confidence Game), Habitual Lying {inclination to lie cannot be resisted even in a situation where an immediate material gain cannot be realized), compulsive lying, Absence of Ethical Conscience.

Note: Types #1 and #2 are passive forms of lying due to tension as seen with contracted forms of writing).

Types #3 and #4 are active forms of lying (due to lack of control as seen with EXPANSIVE exaggeration and formlessness in writing).

Most of us are dishonest to some degree. It is always relative to something and our standards are cultural.

Regarding adolescent anti-social behavior, hopefully, as they mature they "grow out of it." They will test the limits, are narcissistic. In underclass groups, many feel o.k.to be dishonest as long as you don't do it to your own. In Mafia-type groups (or tribal units), the standards are set by the group. Circumstances are important and you must put interpretation in context.

Mendel (206) refers to counter strokes as the manifestation of amorality. The stress of the stroke is on the "counter" quality, the contrariness. It may be an opening where a continuous line is required, an arcade instead of a garland, a left tending stroke instead of a right, a downstroke when an upstroke is correct, etc.

Dishonesty is not always a reason for not employing—it depends upon the situation. There is a fine line between shaving things through omission and outright dishonesty. One needs a sense of the gestalt when determining dishonesty—the overall impression gives a sense of dishonesty. At least four indicators should be present in the handwriting before drawing any conclusions

Illustrations appear on the following pages

#1 - Clear, open, good rhythm (fairly high personal standards), integrity. Productive, active, involved, feels good about self; no need to be dishonest. Irregular spacing indicates there could be some manipulation.

Ellie and Ray Jacobs
are enthusiastic about
your work, and I am
looking forward to seeing
the results of your meeting
with Bill.

#2 - 40-F, Artist. Garland reflects interest in others.

My Pet - I have such a passion for junkmail (what a misdirected passion!) but I saw this and thought of you and Felix - So - how are you?

Love,

and.....

Happy Valentine's Day, your "maîtresse"

you old ...... So and so

#3 a, b - F-33. Retracing, left-terminals (especially in 'b') - oral, take care of me, feed me. Cover strokes (downstrokes covered by upstrokes in MZ indicate hiding, avoiding, protecting, inhibitions.

It is not only astrologers who bang on about you being little homemakers; partners and loved ones are probably asking what happened to that gentle, warm, and tender soul you use to be.

For a start, you can tell them that after three years of utter hell while Saturn was passing through your birth sign, you discovered many things - one of which is heaven not only helps him who helps himself, it also helps him to keep what he to lo...

#4 - Some cover strokes in LZ which slows this incredibly fast handwriting. An expedient stock broker. Angles + thread = exploitation. Low ego + desire and drive = intolerant for blame. The g with angled extension to right indicates psycho logical sophistication. Uses knowledge for own purposes.

Jenny, You always want
to be right and quick to
criticise others involved –
a little bit of knowledge
on this aspect of spot month
dealing might have saved
us negating our commissions
with interest contr or
alternatively embarrassment
opposite clts.

#5 - MZ - hides feelings, efficient, intelligent, business activity, calculated risk taker.

I received the attached since Sadie's mail comes to me.

It looks like they haven't changed the name on the account. Could you pls make sure they change the name, address and social security number on the acct. to Roger Rubin etc. Let me know if you don't have a death certificate, & I'll send you one.

If you don't change, Sadie's going to be taxed with the interest income. Thanks. Rgds,

#6 - F-60. MZ counter strokes. Vitality indicated in business woman's handwriting. The retraced 'o' in "love" (and other oval letters) hides and restricts, has a limited capacity for caring. Ending strokes come back to self. She gives the impression of friendliness, but there is a high level of insincerity. She doesn't want to be restricted. She will turn things around and rationalize so that other is to blame. It is an emotional handwriting, but not caring. She is likely to weep and carry on and then blame--she gets from others what her own parents neglected to give her.

We love you
and wish you
many more happy
birthday's to come..
Hope you enjoy
using your gift -
and now we can
really communicate
often - - - we love
you - - - Mom
+ George

#7 - Slow, lack of spontaneity, takes time to deliberate. Criminals often write slow. Can be a sign of low intelligence. Oral, rounded handwriting an indication of childishness; first priority is comfort. Need for stimulation. Lack of will power, yields to needs, undisciplined. A waitress, died of cancer in her 30s.

-1 Its 8:00 am and I'm re
this letter. I waited till the
as usual and I told you I'd
over by ten. I have a cold
to stay home today.
I have recently married
very happy. My husband is
I love him very much. I am
of another war, for purely se
I would hate to have Jimmi
to be drafted and taken awa
Pretty strange - right! I usual
look on the bright side of thin
I work as a waitress part-tim

#8 - Scattered, no focus, lives by impulses. Internal controls are limited, so he is easily tempted. Won't carefully plan large capers. Gay, drug abuse. Probably had much physical, emotional, psychological abuse in childhood. Space, form, and movement are all disturbed. Many counter strokes.

Jeannie, Carolyn,
Morgan & myself went
out for a bite to eat.
We will be
going to Jilly's (not
Baby Face) it is at
1426A Bishop St. Please,
if you're not too tired—
try and join us.

Forever,
Trish

P.S.
We will
be at
Jilly's

#9 - Good space and rhythm and movement; high intelligence. Editor of a medical magazine. Wife married the handwriting; writer a cross dresser, wrote bad checks, alcoholic. Rather rigid and artificial, persona handwriting (but what is the question).

Many thanks for that very
clipping. It's true without
with high protein + minera
there just isn't any feel
for alcohol; hunger, hi-C
turns the mind in that.

At present I'm especially
this not being able to e.
all. Even so I've managed
since those first days in t.
through will power, partly A
plain lack of cash! Comm
awareness also helps and
helps to reinforce common s
at a time that I need all

So, many many thanks.

#10 - F-40. Well-known psychic. Secondary thread, neglect of form which limits movement. When neglected, like this, doesn't observe rules, untrustworthy. Capitals where they don't belong show confused values.

Roger please phone and
let me Know. what
is doing with you?
How are you and your love
life?
Smile

#11 – Sex worker, drug addict, found religion. No tolerance for delay, needs immediate gratification. Handwriting primitive, neglected and undeveloped.

Where would you like to Go on a trip?

Ha Ha,

How about Hawaii

One Thing Someone Has to Say to You, You do Good work.

#12 - M-40. Lawyer. Profession has the best and worst and he's one of the worst. Wide word space means terrified of intimacy. The capitals are out of proportion showing a weak ego. Clever, smart, manipulative. Overall organization okay.

Attached are copies of the face and other pertinent pages of Mary and my various insurance policies and what changes you think we should be making.

Let me know if you need any additional info. Mary intends to follow through with NYLIC regarding my "retirement" coverage.

Best Regards

#13 - Ronald Reagan. Takes the easy way out; avoids forms.

I believe the Bible is the result of Divine inspiration & is not just a history. I believe in it 13

Ronald Reagan RR

Ronald Reagan

I was raised in the Christian Church which as you know believes in baptism when the

I make only one promise and I make it to myself as well as to you I will not soften

#14 - M-19 overly round, poor rhythm, unusual emphasis on LZ. Resistant, aggressive, rigid.

Dear Roger,
As I sit here writing this letter to you, I wonder if the writing is write, beacause I can't rember the last time when I script.
Anyway I hope this will help you complete my writing analysis.
Well thats it for now, and I will see you on Thursday.

#15 F-24 - Girlfriend of 55-yr old artist. Was severely beaten by mother as a child.

Dear Roger,
I'm really nervous about writing my letter to you. I'm not sure if this is a good enough sample of my writing. When I spoke to you on the phone I was really crazy I'm like that when I'm nervous like when I get to the bottom of the page and can't move my hand as much.

#16 - Artificial handwriting, persona, hypocrisy. Dishonesty is more in relationships. Extremely insecure, hugs baseline. Narrow letters with wide spaces giving impression of something she isn't. Roman (99) notes that this contradiction indicates caution and restraint and is typical of the American girl who displays initiative and effectiveness in her outward activities, but is inhibited in emotional expression. The rigid handwriting shows that she is stuck in a pattern.

Hi! Would you
be interested in meeting a
girl to whom you wrote
quite a while ago, who for
certain reasons couldn't
answer you at that time?
Please accept my apologies.
My name is [illegible] Zorel
and I used to be No.
P-2005 in The Black Book.
When I received
your letter, I was deep in
an involvement which
led to quite a lengthy
relationship. That however
has passed and I'm now
writing to see if you'd be

#17 - Rabbi

t tribes are buried. The Angel Moroni said that the religions of today are wrong... He was told to establish the Latter Day Saints. They moved to Ohio then to Ill. and then to ... Here they received a charter the City Navarro. Smith and Young led it as a theocracy. Joseph Smith was killed in a riot. Brigham Young succeeded and took his people to Utah ... of earnings are contributed to church. ... was the result of reading ... travels. In 1846 they deserted Navarro. They left in groups. The first group consisted of 300 wagons. They established ... stations, planted crops and laid out the location ... after the first group 15,000 people many in groups crossed the desert at the Platt River they built a ferry

#18

Infinite Thinker Thinking within Itself upon Itself about Itself

2. WHAT DOES RELIGIOUS SCIENCE MEAN BY THE TERM SUBCONSCIOUS MIND?

It is the subjective expression of the of the acting out of the laws of the concious mind or spirit in the individual.

has completed UNIT No. One in the FIRST YEAR COURSE in the SCIENCE OF MIND, recommended and accredited by the International Association of Religious Science Churches.

Minister

#19 - Salesman. Sadistic, social problems, paranoia easily stimulates. Extremes in handwriting always signals something is out of balance.

#20

Some other aspect of my
handwriting that others see too?
Sometimes (I'm not doing
it now because I'm thinking
about it.) I will write
an "m" and I'll actually
get an "n" or "rn" which I
usually amend to "m." What
are the psychological reasons
behind this, I wonder.
I also notice sometimes

#21 - Male-40. Male handwriting that looks feminine. Artificial, "perfect" handwriting, rigid. Good boy who turned bad. Lives isolated life, grows own food, no reality testing (doesn't share the same reality as others).

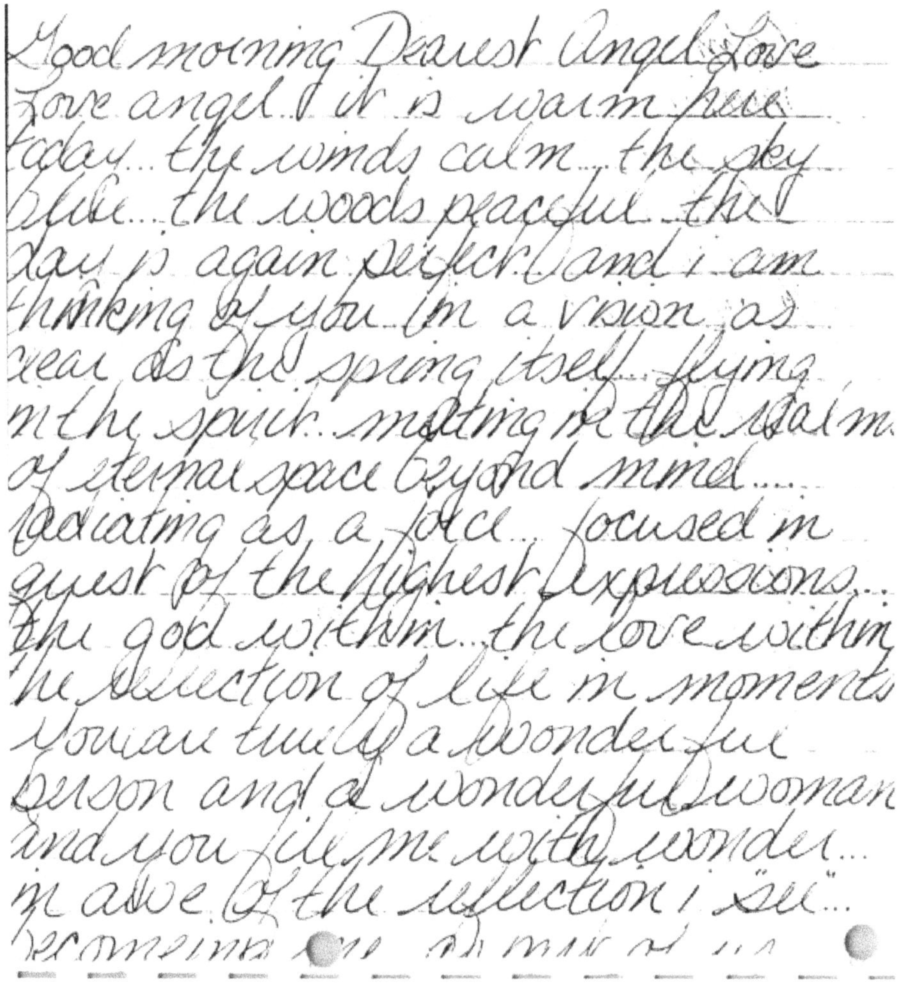
Good morning Dearest Angel Love
Love angel I it is warm here
today... the winds calm... the sky
blue... the woods peaceful... the
day is again perfect and i am
thinking of you in a vision as
clear as the spring itself... flying
in the spirit... melting in the realm
of eternal space beyond mind....
radiating as a force... focused in
quest of the Highest Expressions...
the god within... the love within
the reflection of life in moments
You are truly a wonderful
person and a wonderful woman
and you fill me with wonder...
in awe of the reflection i "see"...

#22 - No resistance, drug dealer, no limits, intelligent but unable to use it constructively.

Today's lunch was extremely light. I had stuffed filet of sole, a salad, white wine, and the most delicious fresh fruit for desert.

#23 - Gives in to impulses, no definition, irregular forms, and pressure.

13. Fear. #1

I may lose my house.
won't be able to pay the
gardener, temple, electric Bill,
Tel etc. My business
is certainly going out
after sixteen years. I
am going to run out
of gas. Tomorrow the bank
& the Tax man will be
after me. Some one will
tell my Family what I
did when I was
drinking & it may
present a lot of

#24 - F-23

I'd like to write words for a new world. I'd like to be able to invent the most beautyful clouds, and strangest rainbows and magic things and to be able to put them in words to give you.

I'd like to have the power of changing the everyday's life, to recreate a beginning: I took my life in my hands and I looked at it: what do I have to give? Not clouds, not rainbows, not blues skies: all I have is fears, sadness, solitude, and the streets and early mornings, when it's still dark and look: my life had to grow up in a hurrie, got to know reality by kicks in the face, I know what "hurt" means and what needing someone desperately feels like, and I'm learning very slowly to ask, to need and to say so.

Can you help me to open my eyes and teach them to understand what's written in this old heart of mine? Help me to take away from it the anxiety of nights spent running, afraid of being late of not finding anybody. Help me to

#25 - F-30

As per our telephone conversation; here is a a sample of my handwriting.

I am in the midst of creating songs for my second album. It is hard for me to create sometimes because I am unable to play an instrument or write music.

I am capable of creating with my lead guitarist — Jimmy Crespo — we are capable of spontaneity (I didn't spell this correct, I know!) A sample of his handwriting is submitted (phone, it is extremely personal) Flame, as a band, is extremely harm

#26 -

Dear Roger,

Well my cold has gone and I feel well. How have you been? Be good to see you,

XX Carl

#27 - M-46

26

Dear Roger,
~~A friend has~~ Two friends have gone to Europe and left ~~her~~ their dog and cat for my daughter and ~~her~~ to take care of in trade for their loft apt. My daughter has just finished boarding school and she is going to live near me for at least a year. She is 17. My life is changing a lot. Tings seem

#28 - M-33

Dear Roger

a lot has been happening to Susanna and I lately and we keep referring to the tape of her session with you which includes many references to me. I would be very grateful if you could find time to see me before Xmas

#29

I approach this meeting with anticipation and and some skeptisism, over the last two years I have gone through many changes all leading in a direction; I don't ~~to~~ know where

#30 - Unusual x in "Dear Michael." That is rare for a man to do. Overblown

TOYOTA
VOLVO
ISUZU

Jan 18, 1990

Dear Michael:

Please accept lease with my most sincere apologies – I have no excuse.

# Write Choice Ink books

Advanced Studies in Handwriting Psychology, Collected Works of:

Jeanette Farmer

Terry Henley

Renate Griffiths

Sheila Lowe

Shirl Solomon

**And, coming early 2025**

Sr. June Canoles

Roger Rubin

# Non-fiction books by Sheila Lowe

*Reading Between the Lines: Decoding Handwriting*

*Advanced Studies in Handwriting Psychology*

*Personality & Anxiety Disorders*

*Succeeding in the Business of Handwriting Analysis*

*Improve Your Life with Graphotherapy*

*Handwriting of the Famous & Infamous*

*The Complete Idiot's Guide to Handwriting Analysis*

*Sheila Lowe's Handwriting Analyzer software*

MEMOIR

*Growing From the Ashes*

# About the Editor

Sheila Lowe is a forensic handwriting examiner and graphologist. She holds a Master of Science degree in psychology.

President of the American Handwriting Analysis Foundation and Ethics Chair for the Scientific Association of Forensic Examiners, she has taught handwriting examination at the University of California Riverside Campus in the CSI Certificate program, and at UC Santa Barbara in the international Discovery program.

Sheila is the author of numerous internationally acclaimed nonfiction books dealing with handwriting and personality, and two fiction series, and her Handwriting Analyzer software has been used around the world since 1997. Sheila Lowe serves an international clientele includes mental health professionals, attorneys, private investigators, staffing agencies, and many others.

www.sheilalowe.com
www.sheilalowebooks.com

facebook.com/SheilaLoweBooks
twitter.com/Sheila_Lowe
instagram.com/SheilaLoweBooks
bookbub.com/authors/sheila-lowe
goodreads.com/sheilalowe
linkedin.com/in/sheilalowe

## FICTION WORKS BY SHEILA LOWE

CLAUDIA ROSE NOVELS

*Poison Pen*

*Written In Blood*

*Dead Write*

*Last Writes*

*Inkslingers Ball*

*Outside The Lines*

*Written Off*

*Dead Letters*

*Maximum Pressure*

BEYOND THE VEIL NOVELS

*What She Saw*

*Proof Of Life*

*The Last Door*

www.ingramcontent.com/pod-product-compliance
Lightning Source LLC
Chambersburg PA
CBHW062048270326
41931CB00013B/2985

* 9 7 8 1 9 7 0 1 8 1 5 5 5 *